FIRED!

BY GOD AND MAN

TOM NAFZIGER

ENDORSEMENTS

I recommend to you, *FIRED! By God and Man*, a powerful book by Pastor Tom Nafziger that will challenge you to pursue a more intimate relationship with Jesus Christ, to move beyond casual acquaintance to mature discipleship. It is not a second-hand account, but personal experiences of a man who is totally sold out to Jesus. Pastor Tom was led by the Spirit to break through long-established racial, social and denominational barriers, and his creative ways of sharing the Gospel will encourage, instruct and inspire you to exercise bold faith. Pastor Tom and his wife Shirley have a long track record of effective ministry and leading many to the Savior. Through a myriad of unusual circumstances, they have learned that God is faithful in the best and worst circumstances. Although they have been blessed with numerous mountain-top experiences, they have demonstrated how to trust God in deep adversity and uncertainty. In his humble, unassuming manner, Pastor Tom sees obstacles as opportunities to rely upon the power of God to perform miracles. Read this engaging and fascinating account of how God used two very ordinary people in extraordinary ways because of their passion for souls and willingness to obey Him. You will be encouraged to aspire to be all that God has called you to be and to attempt the "impossible" as you rely upon the God with whom all things are possible.

Angie B. Williams
Ordained Mennonite minister
Interdenominational Bible teacher
Author of the book, *Joy In Adversity*

This inspiring book, *FIRED! By God and Man*, by Tom Nafziger, is a remarkable read of his walk in faith. God in grace has called the several of us from simple farm backgrounds in Ohio and enabled us to serve Him in many ways, at home and abroad.

The Scripture says that the Holy Spirit "gives us gifts individually as He wills," so this is not the same for each of us. While the witness of the Spirit in this writing may differ from the Spirit's witness in others of us, the same Spirit of Jesus engages us with integrity and joy in the discipleship of Christ.

The emphasis of this book calls us to join in presenting Jesus as LORD and in calling people to become participants in the Kingdom of God with all of His priorities for life.

Dr. Myron S. Augsburger
President Emeritus of Eastern Mennonite College and Seminary
International evangelist
Former pastor of Tuttle Mennonite Church of Sarasota, Florida
Author of over twenty books
Distinguished lecturer

It is rare that you see a person with four children give up their vocation and change their complete lifestyle to serve the LORD.... As you read this book, you will find that life for Tom and his family was not easy, but you will get a glimpse of what God can do when you are sold out to Him.

Bud Hitt
Retired businessman
Archbold, Ohio

It took an amazing wife to leave home with four young children in tow to follow Tom in his pursuit to serve the LORD. But, we have an amazing God.

Gertrude Hitt
Archbold, Ohio

Be prepared not to be able to put this book down. We are honored to call this man of God our friend.

Dr. & Mrs. Paul Ritter
Bradenton, Florida

If you want your faith built, if you want to learn how to follow the Spirit, if you want proof of God's intervention in the lives of those who trust Him, read Tom Nafziger's book, *FIRED! By God and Man.* This is more than a personal testimony; this is a testimony verifying the reality of the LORD Jesus Christ. Remember, "The testimony of Jesus is the spirit of prophecy" (Rev. 19:20). Reading about what God 'has done' ("the testimony of Jesus") is an automatic revelation of what He 'can still do' for those who believe ("the spirit of prophecy").

Mike Shreve
Founder/Director of Deeper Revelation Books
Author, Itinerant speaker
Cleveland, Tennessee

This erudite, eloquent and immensely thought-provoking work is indispensable reading for anyone who wants to live life above the norm. This is a profound authoritative work that could possibly become a classic in this and the next generation.

This exceptional work by Tom Nafziger is one of the most profound, practical, principle-centered approaches to the subject of personal discovery I have read in a long time. The author's approach to this timely issue brings a fresh breath of air that captivates the heart, engages the mind and inspires the spirit of the reader.

The author's ability to leap over complicated theological and metaphysical jargon and reduce complex theories to simple practical principles that the least among us can understand is amazing.

This work will challenge the intellectual while embracing the laymen as it dismantles the mysterious of the soul search of mankind and delivers the profound in simplicity. The author also integrates in each chapter the time-tested precepts giving each principle a practical application to life making the entire process people-friendly.

Every sentence of this book is pregnant with wisdom and I enjoyed the mind-expanding experience of this exciting book. I admonish you to plunge into this ocean of knowledge and watch your life change for the better.

Dr. Myles Munroe
Founder: Myles Munroe International
BFM International
ITWL Association
Nassau Bahamas

All Scripture quotations, except for Appendix #1 or when otherwise indicated, are taken from the: **New King James Version**®. Copyright © 1982 by Thomas Nelson, Inc. Used by permission. All rights reserved.

Other Scripture references are from the following sources:
King James Version (KJV) public domain.
New International Version® (NIV). Copyright © 1973, 1978, 1984 International Bible Society. Used by permission of Zondervan. All rights reserved.
New American Standard Bible (NASB), Scripture quotations taken from the New American Standard Bible®, Copyright © 1960, 1962, 1963, 1968, 1971, 1972, 1973, 1975, 1977, 1995 by The Lockman Foundation. Used by permission. (www.Lockman.org)

Cover Design by Jeff Johnson www.j2arts.com; book layout and design by Bunny Bateman.

In all versions, personal pronouns referring to God (except for "who"or "whom") have been capitalized, to stay consistent with the rest of the text and most importantly, to give honor to the Most High.

Publisher's Cataloging-in-Publication
(Provided by Quality Books, Inc.)
Nafziger, Tom.

Fired! : by God and man / Tom Nafziger.
p. cm.
LCCN 2010943452
ISBN-13: 978-0-942507-14-0
ISBN-10: 0-942507-14-2
  1. Nafziger, Tom. 2. Clergy—Biography—Anecdotes.
3. Christian biography—Anecdotes. 4. Spiritual life—
Christianity—Anecdotes. I. Title.
BV4015.N34 2011   253
  QBI11-600001

Send all personal correspondence to:
Tom Nafziger
c/o Christian Retreat, 1200 Glory Way Blvd., Bradenton, FL 34212
Phone: 803-571-0784 Email: cffpastor@yahoo.com

Published by **Deeper Revelation Books**
Revealing "the deep things of God" (1 Cor. 2:10)
P.O. Box 4260, Cleveland, TN 37320
Phone: 423-478-2843
Email: info@deeperrevelationbooks.org
Website: www.deeperrevelationbooks.org
Visit our website for distribution information and a listing of other DRB products.

DEDICATION

I dedicate this book to Shirley, my dear wife of forty-five years, who has stood by me through everything. I am so grateful.

To my parents, Lester and Marjorie Nafziger; I can never thank them enough for raising me in "the nurture and admonition of the LORD" and for their examples of true, dedicated Christian lives (Eph 6:4). God blessed them with seventy years of marriage together.

To my brothers and sisters, that through this book they will be able to understand more perfectly the events that happened in my life.

To our children, Tyler, Tony, Todd and April, who experienced some intense challenges as they walked through the changes in our lives. And to all our grandchildren and great-grandchildren whom I pray will benefit from this work. I dedicate this book to all who read it, that it might be a blessing in their lives and urge them on to a deeper walk with God.

ACKNOWLEDGMENTS

I acknowledge my Savior and my LORD Jesus the Christ without whom I am nothing.

I acknowledge with thanks all who have made deposits in my life and have encouraged and prayed for me throughout my journey with God, especially Bud and Gertrude Hitt, my 'spiritual parents,' and also Brother Gerald and Sister Beulah Derstine whom I am delighted to have as my pastors. Others include Reverend Bob Armstrong who helped guide and encourage me in putting it all together. A special thanks to Terry JoAnn Beck who contributed greatly to the editing process.

I especially want to acknowledge my wife, Shirley, who had to put up with me when I seemed to be in another world while writing this book.

God bless each and every one.

Thomas Eugene Nafziger

TABLE OF CONTENTS

FOREWORD

If you ever wonder what it might be like to step out on faith, *Fired! By God and Man* by author Tom Nafziger will give you an illuminating illustration and understanding. I am personally acquainted with the author and can assure you this book will not bore you. It will keep you in awe as to how God can see you through some of the most amazing situations. The transparency that Tom displays in this writing will surely bring answers to many of your preconceived fears in relation to what it must be like to trust in God.

The author in this writing currently reveals a very highly fulfilled life. He has walked out his faith and continues to do so, thus he is able to encourage so many other young hopefuls ready to step out into ministry.

This story will challenge you, as well as encourage you to be also willing to step out on your faith and do it! With God, all things are possible. God will allow you to see the world and discover that your life will make a difference in the lives of the multitudes that you encounter. God does equip you and prods you to 'just do it.' Today, Tom is a legend in the minds of those who personally know him.

Both negatives and positives may manifest in your walk with God, but happily, we know the negatives ultimately translate into the final positive, "Well done, thou good and faithful servant!" Take your time reading the contents of this book and meditate on the many awesome experiences. It could very well be your turn next!

Gerald G. Derstine,
Founder, President, Strawberry Lake Christian Retreat
Founder, Gospel Crusade Ministerial Fellowship
Co-Founder, Gospel Crusade, Inc.
Director, Israel Affairs International

INTRODUCTION

In Genesis 12:1, we read, "Now the LORD had said to Abram, 'Get out of your country, from your family and from your father's house, to a land that I will show you.'" How did Abram know it was God speaking? He had not heard God speak before this instance. Neither did he know where he was going nor what was in store for him. God led him through the wilderness to a land he knew not. God blessed him beyond all expectations because of his obedience to go wherever he was sent.

You will read in these pages of how God spoke to Tom Nafziger on February 24, 1979, in the Fulton County Jail in Wauseon, Ohio. God challenged him to go. Where? He did not know. Yet he did know, before hearing the voice of God, that he was unwilling to become a missionary and go to Africa.

Tom was raised in a modest income Mennonite home in northwest Ohio, never believing that he would travel around the world someday. Not unlike many others, Tom held in reserve an area of his life that prevented God from accomplishing His very best in him. Although he tried many different jobs looking for fulfillment, only when Tom took off all the restraints did he begin to enjoy life truly to its fullest.

You will read many of the supernatural experiences that can accompany anyone totally sold out to obeying God's will for his or her life.

Shirley Nafziger

Chapter 1

A VOICE FROM HEAVEN

"When was the last time you prayed for your enemies?" These words startled me and penetrated my very innermost being. However, I immediately knew 'Who' was asking the question. It was God Himself! How did I know that? I'm not sure, I just knew. Let me tell you, when God speaks to you, you will just know!

That question was soon followed by the second one, **"Do you see what I can do if you will just go?"** His voice was so powerful and penetrating, yet wonderfully sweet.

So how did I happen to hear these questions? Let me explain. Legend has it that Baby Face Nelsen was once incarcerated in the Fulton County Jail. Until the old building was destroyed to make room for the new one, the bullet holes in the red brick walls were still visible from when his gang tried to bust him out. As interesting as that may be, going to this cold dark jail was never my idea of a good time. But I digress....

It started with my association with Gideons International, a group of business and professional men committed to the distribution of copies of the Bible, God's Word, to fifth-grade children in schools, doctor's offices, hotels and around the world. I had joined this association with all of the wrong motives. My plan was, I thought, to get to know other businessmen, which in turn would help my business grow, thus allowing me to accomplish my goals in life—get rich, retire by the age of forty and then go fishing and golfing for the rest of my life. Knowing what I now know, I would have been so bored.

While in the hardware business, I met an unusual man, Bud Hitt. He would come into the hardware store from time to time to get some supplies for his trophy manufacturing business. He was also a member of the Gideons.

[My plan was working.] It seemed that every time he would come in, he had a story to tell of how he had led someone to the LORD in the course of his daily life. In fact, each time he would say something like, "I picked up a hitch hiker the other day and led him to the LORD," a verse of scripture would float through my mind like one of those huge letter banners they pull behind an airplane, "By their fruits you will know them" (Mt 7:20). However, I had no fruit. When fruit like an apple grows on a tree it is not fully fruit until it is ripe. Ripe fruit does no good until it is picked. Picked ripe fruit still does not fulfill its purpose until it is offered as food to someone. At that time, it seemed to me that true fruit would only exist in my life if I led someone to the LORD... and I never had.

Bud visited the jail each month. He would hand out Bibles and bring a report to the Gideon meeting. "We led six people to the LORD this month," was often a part of his report. Again, there was that verse in my mind, "By their fruit you shall know them."

On February 23, 1979, Bud came into my store. Since business was slow, we started talking. Of course, it wasn't long until he brought up a story of how he had led another person to the LORD.

I finally admitted to him, "Bud, I am thirty-two years old, and I have never led anyone to the LORD." He didn't condemn me. He just said, "Well, would you like to go with me to the jail tomorrow?" Here was my opportunity. I sure wanted to see him lead another soul to Jesus, so I said, "Okay, I will go and **watch**!" Little did I know what God had in mind for me.

The next morning I opened up the hardware store, informed the other sales clerks there of my plan and went to the jail. As Bud and I entered and proceeded up the steep, cold, dark stairway, we came to the door of the cell where a young man by the name of Gary was staying. Bud had visited him before and had given him a book to read. He asked Gary, "Did you read that book I gave you?" Gary answered, "I sure did." "Well," Bud said, "Would you like to give your heart to Jesus today?" I thought, "This is it! I am going to see someone accept the LORD right now." Yet my hopes were soon dashed when I heard Gary say, "No, I'm not ready yet." I was disappointed. Here I had come along to see someone get saved and he refused. Yet, Bud didn't seem to be bothered by his refusal.

We noticed that Gary looked very sick. In fact, he needed to hold on to the wall as he walked over to the cell door. Bud calmly said, "Can I pray for you? I can see you are sick." Gary put his hand on the food tray opening in the cell door. Bud laid his hand on Gary's hand. I thought, "Well, there is no one here from my church to see this," so I placed my hand on top of Bud's. [You see at my church, when people were sick and asked for prayer, there would be just a general prayer that went something like this, "God we ask that you would give the doctors wisdom." If they were really sick and in the hospital and there was a possibility of them dying, the elders would go to the hospital and anoint them with oil. I knew this because they would tell us about it the next Sunday in the church service. We were not allowed to see them anoint with oil. I don't know why.]

Bud prayed a short, but very bold prayer. [He still has a habit of doing that.] He said, "LORD, I just ask you to heal Gary, right now. Amen!" I thought, "I have never heard anyone pray like that before."

I was disappointed that Gary did not want to accept Jesus as his Savior, but thought, "Maybe I could talk Gary in to accepting Christ. After all I am a great salesman." I had won several sales competitions at jobs in years gone by. So, I said something to Gary. I don't remember exactly what I said, but I will never forget what he said to me. Gary looked out that cell door and into my eyes as though he was looking into my very soul, and said, "My trial is coming up next week and it seems like I am fighting the devil himself." Suddenly I heard myself say something that I had not planned to say. "Well if you are fighting against the devil, do you know how you can win?" I somehow knew immediately that he knew the answer, but he hesitated before he spoke. In sales, I had learned that when you asked for the sale, you needed to keep quiet because the next one to speak 'loses.' In this case, it seemed like an eternity went by. I couldn't think of anything to say or I would have said it. Finally, Gary answered, "Well, Jesus is the only one who can win against the devil." [This is not necessarily true, but at that time, it was what he and I believed.] Again I heard words come out of my mouth, "Well then, wouldn't you like to have Him on your side?" I thought, "That was a good question. Why didn't I think of that?"

Gary was no longer able to resist the call of God and he began to cry and said, "Yes." I didn't know what to do next. I looked up at Bud. He was smiling and said, "Let's pray. He led Gary in what we call the Sinner's Prayer. Gary said, "Jesus, come into my heart. I confess that I have sinned and I need You in my life to save me." That is all it took, but Gary didn't stop praying. [I couldn't explain what happened next for quite some time.] He went on, "And LORD, I want to pray for those that I will be in trial against next week." I was absolutely stunned! He had just said earlier they were being used by the devil himself and now he was praying for them. Surprisingly, I heard God ask me two questions.

"When was the last time you prayed for your enemies?" Now understand it was just a matter-of-fact question. There was no condemnation in it. The voice was so very real that I thought Bud probably heard it too. I answered only with my thoughts and not out loud. [I can testify that God can hear your thoughts.] I said, "God, I don't even pray for my friends, let alone my enemies." In those days, the only person I usually prayed for was 'me.' "Oh God, get me out of this problem or that problem."

Then God asked me the second question. You see, I had asked Gary two questions and now God was asking me two questions. He said, **"Do you see what I can do if you will just go?"** I immediately answered, "Okay God, I will go." I meant that I would go anywhere He wanted me to go and do anything He wanted me to do. Up until that point, I knew that I wanted to go to Heaven when I died, but I didn't want to go to Africa and be a missionary. In my twisted concept of what God was like, I thought that was what He would **make** me do. I had my plan for my life all figured out. I would become rich, a millionaire by the time I was forty. Then I would move to Florida and go deep sea fishing every day until I was all fished out. At that point, I would go golfing every day. That was my plan and it didn't include being a missionary in Africa. However, that day I totally surrendered to God's will and His plan for my life. If God had told me right then to go home and pack my bags to go to Africa, I was ready. But He didn't say that. He did start to change me though.

My whole life transformed that day—about 11:00 o'clock in the morning of Saturday, February 24, 1979. I rode home with Bud and told him what had taken place between God and me. Later, when I got home to my wife, Shirley, I told her what had happened. I just wanted to tell everyone.

At that time, I was a Sunday school teacher. I can remember well some of my Sunday school teachers. One of them who made a great impact on my life was Gerald Beck. He made 'friendship evangelism' a very exciting concept to me. Gerald told us many stories and then related them to the message that he was trying to teach us. I guess you could call them illustrated sermons. I can just see him and his brother, Ronnie, running across the field chasing after a man that jumped out of his car and took off. The brothers were both very athletic. When they finally caught up with the man, they were able to talk him in to giving himself up to the authorities. They walked in such grace and were able to minister peace to him.

Now, I was the Sunday school teacher and was supposed to teach the young married class at our church. The next day when I was to start the lesson, I opened the lesson help book. It seemed like the pages were blank. I could not read anything. All I could hear in my mind was, "Tell them what happened yesterday. Tell them what happened yesterday." However, that wasn't what we did in Sunday school. Finally, I said, "Let's pray." After I prayed a short prayer, I opened the lesson book again. The pages still seemed blank. I heard it again, "Tell them what happened yesterday. Tell them what happened yesterday." I closed the book and said, "Before we begin the lesson today, let me tell you what happened yesterday." I recounted the story about Gary and of how God had spoken to me. When I finished, to my amazement, I looked around the classroom and nearly every single student had tears in their eyes. I couldn't understand what was happening. I later learned how the anointing of the Holy Spirit would sometimes cause people to cry. I am reminded of the song, "He Washed My Eyes with Tears," written by Ira Stanfill.

> *He washed my eyes with tears that I might see,*
> *The broken heart I have was good for me;*
> *He tore it all apart and looked inside,*
> *He found it full of fear and foolish pride.*
> *He swept away the things that made me blind,*
> *And then I saw the clouds were silver lined;*
> *And now I understand 'twas best for me,*
> *He washed my eyes with tears that I might see.*

> *He washed my eyes with tears that I might see,*
> *The Glory of Himself revealed to me;*
> *I did not know that He had wounded hands,*
> *I saw the blood He spilt upon the sands.*

I saw the marks of shame and wept and cried,
He was my substitute, for me He died;
And now I'm glad He came so tenderly.
And washed my eyes with tears that I might see.

My life was totally changed. I often found myself crying whenever I felt the presence of the LORD. I had a voracious appetite for the Word of God and read my Bible all of the time. It really spoke directly to me. I would sit and watch Jimmy Swaggart on television and just cry and cry. I knew things had changed in a major way when I would rather read my Bible than watch football. Shirley noticed too, but didn't talk about it.

I got involved with the jail ministry on a regular basis. I soon learned of a juvenile facility a short distance away where I was able to get accepted to hold a Bible study. [It was an eye opening experience. What I couldn't figure out was why they had some female guards for these young boys. They even watched them as they took showers! What??? This is absolutely unacceptable policy for our Department of Corrections. There must be an improved moral code established.] I had opportunity to invite the young boys to get to know Jesus. I remember one evening very well. I gave these fellows an invitation for salvation. Several wanted to receive the LORD but did not because of peer pressure. I left the juvenile facility that day with tears streaming down my face. My heart ached, as I desperately wanted to see souls saved.

And then the dreams started.

Chapter 2

LIFE CHANGING DREAMS

Since I was a young boy, I often had dreams. I would sometimes tell my family of my dreams, and they would laugh at me. Like the time I dreamed my brother was squirting me with cement out of a rubber hose. [The concrete pump had not yet been invented.] When I told him what I had dreamed, he said, "Don't you know that it is impossible to squirt concrete?" Do you suppose God might have been showing me that it is possible to invent something like that? God is the God of inventions. You see, the Bible says that dreams and visions are a language of the Holy Spirit. I believe if we would ask God what He is saying to us when we have a dream, we would be surprised that He is actually talking to us.

After my encounter with God at the county jail, my dreams seemed to take on a divine significance. I am fully aware of the fact that some dreams can be from too much pizza, and some dreams we may never understand. Contrast that with other dreams that are so significant they are actually warnings from God. Could it be God guiding our lives? We should pray and inquire of the LORD for interpretation and understanding of them.

Soon afterwards, I dreamed about Joe. I had been praying that God would give me a passion like Bud's for lost souls because it seemed I was missing many opportunities to be a witness for the LORD. I would recognize too late when I should have spoken out.

In my dream, I was riding on a big yellow school bus, seated next to an old man whose clothes were dirty. He had a two-day growth of whiskers on his face. I had a "Four Spiritual Laws" tract in my pocket. I had been introduced to this tract by the Bill Glass Prison Ministry and never went anywhere without it. I took it out and began to explain the plan of salvation to Joe. He listened intently while I showed him the first three laws.

Law Number (1) God loves you and has a wonderful plan for your life.

Law Number (2) All have sinned and fallen short of the Glory of God.

Law Number (3) Jesus came to bridge the gap so that we can receive forgiveness.

Law Number (4) You can receive forgiveness right now if you will just pray this prayer. "LORD Jesus, come into my life. I confess you are my LORD."

However, when I reached the last law, Joe turned to look out the bus window and talked about something else. I would start all over again, only to reach the same results. As we talked, the bus made various stops to let people off. When we came to Joe's stop, instead of letting him off through the front door of the bus, the driver backed up to the edge of a lake that was frozen over with ice. Joe exited the back door of the bus, stepped into the icy cold snow and walked down the bank onto the ice. Suddenly, the ice broke! Joe fell through the ice and drowned. At that point, what seemed like hundreds of other people began to exit the bus out of the back door. They all walked down into the lake and drowned.

I awoke, weeping so much that my pillow was wet. I realized that many people were lost and headed for Hell. I had received what I had asked God for, a passion for lost souls. I wanted to tell every person I met that God loved them, and if they would receive Jesus, He would save them from their sin. I related this dream to Bud the next time I saw him. However, that was not the end of the story.

Only a few days later, a man walked into the store where I was working. I had not seen him before and did not know him, but this was the "Joe" from my dream. I was shaken to my very core when I learned that his name was actually Joe. I knew that I must talk to him about the LORD so I helped him get the supplies he wanted. As he was about to leave, I said to him, "Sir, I had a dream about you recently." It was his turn to be shocked. "You don't even know me," he growled. "How would you have a dream about me?"

I ignored his question and pulled a "Four Spiritual Laws" tract from my pocket. I showed him Laws 1, 2 and 3. He listened intently, just like in the dream. However, when I got to the law that asked him to pray to receive Jesus as his own personal savior, he changed the subject and talked about something else. I tried again and again, producing the same results. I followed him out the door. There on the sidewalk, on the main street of town, I touched his shoulder and prayed for him.

You must understand, this was not like me. I was always told there are two things you should never talk about in business, politics and religion. I agree. The only thing is I was not talking about politics or religion. I was talking to Joe about his eternal destiny.

Joe left. I went back inside the store. However, Joe did not leave my mind.

A couple of nights later, I had another dream. In the dream, I was driving back to town from the direction where Joe lived when a car passed me at a high rate of speed. A short distance down the road I came upon a car accident. There were mangled bodies everywhere... including Joe's. Again, I awoke weeping. I interpreted this dream to mean that Joe was lost and bound for Hell. I asked around, found out where Joe lived and then went to visit him. Again, I tried to explain to him the way of salvation, but he would not receive it.

This situation was so heavy on my mind that I called Bud, shared the dream and asked him if he would go with me to share the good news of the Gospel with Joe. Immediately, he said he would accompany me so I headed over to pick him up. When I arrived at Bud's house, Gertrude, his wife, said, "Let's pray!" After prayer, Bud and I left for Joe's while Gertrude continued a prayer vigil on our behalf.

Joe's house was located on the same property as an auto junk yard. I knocked; Joe opened the door and invited us in but was quick to point out the loaded rifle behind the front door. I barely even took notice. I had something much more important on my mind. There were about a dozen cats and a dog or two running around the house. You can imagine the pungent odor as the cats and dogs obviously did not get a regular walk outside to do their necessary jobs. I am not sure if there was more junk outside or inside the house. He offered chairs, and we sat down. I again went through the plan of salvation. When I asked him, "Joe, would you like to receive Jesus now?" He replied, "I want to, but I can't!" I didn't understand. Then Joe said, "I know there is one thing that even God can't do." He paused, but since we didn't speak he continued, "He can't heal these spurs that I have on the heels of my feet."

There is one thing you never want to do when Bud Hitt is around. Don't say that God can't do something. Immediately Bud said, "Joe, can we pray for you?" Joe nodded, so Bud and I quickly got down on our knees. The carpet was filthy and urine soaked, but we gladly held Joe's smelly feet in our hands. Bud prayed, "God, I ask you to heal these spurs. And LORD, we bind the spirit that has Joe bound and loose him to make the decision that he wants to make. Amen." We looked up at Joe as he lifted his hands and said, "Praise God, I want to do it now!" That night Joe prayed to receive Jesus as his own personal Savior. I think I understand now why Jesus sent the disciples out two by two. We put Joe in contact with a neighbor that said he would disciple him. I think that was the last time I ever saw Joe. However, I expect to see him again one day in Heaven.

I have had many other significant dreams that have proven to be guidance or warnings from God. I will refer to them later in this book. First, let me tell you about my family and my early years.

Chapter 3

GOD CALLS

I was born into a Mennonite family and raised on a dairy farm in northwest Ohio. I had an older brother named Leslie, two older sisters, Suzie and Karen, and two younger brothers, Mike and Lonnie. For as long as I can remember, I was taken to church regularly.

My mom and dad were very godly parents. They lived the life that they taught us. In fact, they mostly taught us by their daily walk and commitment to God. They disciplined us as seemed best to them. (See Hebrews 12:9.) I cannot thank them enough for the examples they were to my siblings and me. I know they were powerful witnesses to their neighbors as well. My dad loved to sing as he drove the tractor working in the fields. I remember one time when he told the neighbor that lived one-quarter mile down the road that he was practicing his singing for the men's chorus in church. The neighbor answered, "I know. I could hear you from my house!" My father had a strong voice and it carried farther than he was aware.

I had cousins, uncles and great uncles that were preachers. One was even a bishop. My aunt and uncle, S. Paul and Vesta Miller, were missionaries to India for more than forty-four years.

I heard the Word taught from the time I was born. I attended Central Mennonite Church in Archbold, Ohio. My pastor, for as long as I could remember as a youth, was Jesse Short. As he would approach the platform for Sunday morning service, he would often turn half way to his seat and bust out in song, "*Blessed Assurance, Jesus is mine, O what a foretaste of Glory Divine.*" He always sang with great gusto. The congregation would come alive also with singing. My wife, who was then Shirley Kolpfenstein, the youngest of the three Klopfenstein Sisters, would go to the nursing home, the jail and to the Cherry Street Mission with Pastor Jesse to sing. She also helped him make weekly radio programs. I remember many times when Jesse would say to me, "Keep on the firing line!" I knew what he meant, but wasn't sure I was even in the battle.

I was ten years old when during some special church services evangelist Myron Augsburger gave an invitation to respond for salvation. I felt God calling me. I raised my hand to respond and accepted Christ sincerely. When I arrived home that night, my mom and dad called me into their bedroom. We knelt by their bed where my dad prayed, thanking God that He had answered their prayers for me. The next day, I was playing under the quilt where my mother and other ladies were quilting. I heard them talking about the meetings that were taking place at our church where several other young people also had raised their hands. One of the women said that my older brother, Leslie, had raised his hand earlier in the week. Another woman asked who had responded last night. They answered, "Tom did." I had not known that my brother gave his life to the LORD earlier in the week. However, the manner in which these ladies discussed my decision the evening before made me think they thought I only responded because my brother had. This experience was a hindrance to me for some time. [We need to be careful what we say.]

As a teenager, I was elected to teach Sunday school for the younger boys. When I was fifteen years old, I noticed Shirley. She was a young girl in our church I thought was pretty sweet. We began dating, and she totally stole my heart. After a couple of years, we talked about marriage. One evening we went to church together when Myron Augsburger was conducting some revival meetings. He was the same evangelist who had spoken the night I accepted the LORD. When he gave the altar call, my heart began to pound. I leaned over to Shirley and told her that I was going to the altar. I had to go. When I got there, I was happy to see that she came with me. On our way out of the church that night, I asked our pastor to pray for me because I felt that God was calling me into the ministry. He assured me he would, but I think it would have benefited me more if he had prayed right then and there. When we got to Shirley's house, I told her parents that I believed God was calling me into the ministry. When I arrived at my house, I also discussed with my parents how I felt God's call on my life. However, I don't think I ever talked about my call again until many years later.

I got busy with my life. Shirley and I made our plans to get married. It was 1965 and the military draft was in effect. Two months before the wedding I received my draft notice. In the Mennonite church, we were taught not to go in the military but to serve our country in an alternate service. I contacted my local draft board. They told me to go ahead with my wedding plans but to enter the service immediately afterward, which I did. We moved to Sarasota, Florida, where I went to work at the Sarasota Memorial Hospital. I remember praying, "LORD, help me to lead at least one person to the LORD in the next two years while I am in the I-W service." Just like after hearing the call into the ministry, I managed to put that desire aside, at least for the most part. One time I tried to say something to an orderly but chickened out. Needless to say, I did not fulfill that prayer. It seemed like I just did not have the power or the boldness to speak up. [As I said earlier, after my encounter with the LORD, all of that changed. Now, I can't stop speaking about the things I have seen and heard.]

When my service time was completed, we had our first child, Tyler E. Nafziger. We immediately moved back to Ohio where I went into the construction business for myself. I thought this was the way to fulfill my goals for life. For a short time, it seemed like things were going well. Yet, it wasn't long until I was totally dissatisfied again. After our second son, Tony E. Nafziger, was born in Ohio, we moved back to Florida again. There is a saying that once you have gotten sand in your shoes you will always return to Florida. However, I was searching for an answer to this yearning in my heart for fulfillment. When you are not obeying God, you will never be satisfied.

We lived in Florida for a few years and our third son, Todd E. Nafziger, was born. We moved back to Ohio and bought a house in Pettisville. Our daughter, April M. Nafziger, was born while we lived there. I travelled throughout Ohio, Michigan and Indiana selling wood ladders and unfinished pine furniture for the Archbold Ladder Company, the company that my grandfather and his brother had owned for many years. My grandfather was my hero. All through the depression, he had provided jobs for many of the residents of Archbold. He made sure I knew that they kept their company in the black financially every year. Their margin of gross profit was one-quarter of a cent per foot of ladder.

During this time, I met a man in a small town in Ohio who was on fire for Jesus. I shared some of my frustrations and found myself praying with him on my knees next to a sofa in his place of business. Somehow, I thought that if I owned my own business, I could accomplish my goals in life. I heard about a small business that was for sale and began planning to buy it. There was also a larger hardware store in Archbold, Ohio, that I thought might be for sale. I was able to buy stock in the company that owned that store and later bought more until I had the majority ownership. At that time, I became the manager and was on my way to meeting my goal of becoming rich, or at least I thought so.

I got real busy making changes in the operation of the store, cleaning up some of the property around the store and generally making some waves. It was at this time I decided that if I joined some kind of an organization, I would get to know more business people and would build my business faster. I chose the Gideons and joined with the express purpose of using it to build my empire. That was when I met Bud Hitt. Some people said Bud was a fanatic. I later heard a definition that a fanatic for Jesus is anyone who loves Jesus more than you do.

I had been warned to stay away from Bud because he was peculiar. I was told that if you got too close to him 'something' might jump on you, making you peculiar too. I discovered they were somewhat correct, only it was not 'something,' rather it was 'Some One.' Furthermore, He does not 'jump' on you. However, He will come and dwell with you and empower you when you invite Him in.

I tried to be cautious, but Bud didn't do anything except show God's love to me. I admired his life and even found myself drawn toward him. He talked about Jesus every time I saw him.

At that time, I experienced some financial challenges in the business. Some of the stockholders wanted me to participate in practices that I believed would leave a poor testimony. When I refused to go along, it became apparent that I needed to separate myself from those men. I began preparations to buy their stock. Instead, they purchased my stock, setting me free to pursue God's call on my life.

I was the deputy registrar in our area, issuing license plates for cars, trucks and trailers, etc. I moved that aspect of the business to another location where Shirley and I continued it. This gave me time to study my Bible for many hours between customers. God supernaturally provided financially for us. Later, I took a third-shift job as the foreman at the same ladder factory where I had worked previously as a salesman. I remember one evening in particular. I had a special encounter with the LORD as I was preparing to go to work. Each night when I arrived at the factory, I would receive my instructions from the second-shift foreman. But on this evening, I don't recall what he asked me or what my reply was. However, I do remember that I saw tears well up in his eyes as he was touched by the anointing that I was still experiencing from my time with the LORD.

I had recently entered into the experience of the Baptism of the Holy Spirit and had spoken in tongues. Still, I was having a real mental battle with the whole experience. One night I determined to find out if this thing of speaking in tongues was for real or not. While the machines were running and no one could hear, I spoke in tongues for about seven or eight hours. In the morning, I had no more doubts.

God never gives up on us. He will confirm His word to us if we will trust and obey Him. I was so hungry for God and the yearning for a deeper relationship was growing more and more intense.

One day, as I was thinking about all that was taking place in my life, I heard a voice. The voice told me that Shirley and our four children were going to die so that I would be free to evangelize all around the world. I thought it was God and reluctantly said, "Well God, that is very hard, but if that is what You have chosen for me, then, okay." However, I became more and more depressed as days went by. Shirley noticed that I wasn't acting like myself and asked me what was wrong. How do you tell someone you love more than any other person on this earth that she was going to die? I couldn't do it.

Deeper and deeper I went into depression. Finally Shirley said, "Why don't you call Bud and talk to him?" I was desperate. It sounded like a good idea... until we met. I felt even more frustrated as I searched for words to explain it to him. Finally, I just blurted it out, "Bud, God told me that He is going to kill Shirley and our children so I can go wherever He wants me to go." Having started, I couldn't stop the torrent of words and told him everything. He listened for a while and suddenly stopped me with sharp words, "Satan I rebuke you!" He then commanded the devil to take his hands off me and set me free from the depression.

I was shocked! I had not heard Bud talk this way before. I was completely unaware of the fact that I had been deceived by this attack from the enemy. The amazing thing is that I was suddenly and completely relieved and set free.

I thank God for this friend who is also a spiritual father to me. Never be afraid to confide in those around you who love you. They are sent by God to help you.

Chapter 4

INSTALLMENT PRISON TIME

After my encounter with God, I was reminded of my call to the ministry. The Bill Glass Prison Ministry was having a rally at a local restaurant. I had heard about that ministry before and decided to go. That night they announced that their next crusade was scheduled for Texas. Without hesitation, I made a commitment to go.

The night before I was to leave, my mom and dad came to our house to see me. When they came in, we began walking into the living room when my dad said he wanted to see me alone first. Shirley and my mom went on ahead into the room. My dad handed me a check. He had tears in his eyes as he told me, "Your mother and I made a commitment to God before you were born that if any of our children ever went into the ministry, we would help them." That was the first offering I ever received for ministry. I was flabbergasted! I had never thought about people giving me money or offerings for sharing my testimony and leading others to Jesus.

My dad had always been a giver, though he never talked about it much. However, when he spoke of his sister who served as a missionary to India for many years, I could tell that he had helped her more than once. I have a wonderful heritage in the faith and am exceedingly grateful for it.

The trip to Texas was an awesome experience. We sang, prayed and just talked a whole lot about Jesus. I met Sam Wenger on this trip. He was a Mennonite pastor who was different. His church was growing rapidly because people that did not have a Mennonite name were being saved and joining the church. Sam and I were driving during the night. One of us drove while the other rode shot gun, then we would switch. The time flew by as we shared our testimonies with each other. This was just a precursor for what was to come once we got to the prison.

Sam and I attended the Bill Glass Prison Crusade's orientation meeting the first night as 'freshman counselors.' The next day we were to go into the prison and speak one-on-one with the inmates about Jesus. We all used the "Four Spiritual Laws" tract for the plan of salvation. [You will find this tract reprinted in the back of this book.] This was done so if more than one counselor talked to the same inmate, the prisoner heard the same approach. I led ten men to the LORD during that weekend. I was so 'high,' I didn't want to come down. Sam told me he was shocked as he watched me in the prison. He said every time he saw me, I had an inmate backed up into a corner and was sharing the Gospel with him. I don't think I backed them into a corner. However, I was thrilled that so many were hungry to hear the good news. It was sort of like fishing in a barrel with 2000 fish in it and they were all starving. One of the celebrities who spoke at these crusades would often say, "I am just a beggar who has found a piece of bread and am willing to share it with another beggar." On our return to Ohio, we shared Jesus with people in restaurants and gas stations and several gave their hearts to the LORD.

I tried to settle back into my work again. However, since I had tasted of ministering the Word of God, it wasn't the same. A couple of weeks later, as I was getting dressed one morning, I noticed a lump about the size of an egg under my left arm. I thought, "That's strange." What was strange was that although I knew that the lump was a sign of cancer, I had absolutely no fear. The Scripture says, "Perfect love casts out fear" (I Jn 4:8).

When I told my mother about the lump she immediately said, "You get to a doctor." Well you know how mothers are... I went to the doctor. When the doctor looked at the lump, he asked if I had been scratched by a cat. I told him, "No." Then he very calmly replied, "It is probably just a fatty tumor. But let's take it out and know for sure." My first thought was, "I wonder who needs to get saved at the hospital." I figured that must be why God would send me there. After the surgery, as I was waking up from the anesthesia, the doctor came into my room. He took hold of my toe, wiggled it and said, "Well, it was cancer but we are sending it off to determine what type." Again I thought, "Well there must be someone else who needs to hear the Gospel."

The next day, Bud and Sam came to my room to pray for me. I wondered how they found out so soon that I was in the hospital. I didn't know for many months that Shirley had called Carol, a friend of ours, and asked her to call Bud. You see, Shirley was having some problems with my change. She seemed to be afraid of Bud and my newfound friends. She later shared with me her reaction to my announcement of how I felt God calling me to ministry while we were still dating. Shirley explained that she didn't want to be the wife of a preacher. Yet, here I was… heading in that direction. Bud and Sam prayed the healing prayer of faith. They left a couple of Kathryn Kuhlman books with me to read and left my hospital room. As I read the books, tears ran down my cheeks as the presence of the LORD became so real. Those books told of God's healing power and many testimonies of specific healings and miracles. It built my faith.

When the report came back from the pathology lab, it read that I had Hodgkin's disease, a form of lymphoma. I did not have any doubts or fear of dying. The doctors ran several tests including a lymph angiogram where they made a small cut in the top of my feet and injected dye into the lymph system. Then they x-rayed my body to see if the cancer had spread. They found nothing but said I definitely still had cancer. After consultation, they determined that I should have twenty-three cobalt radiation treatments. My faith was growing but had not reached the level where I could claim my total healing. I consented to the treatments.

Several people volunteered to drive me to Toledo for the treatments. One day Bud took me. My hair had started to fall out from the radiation. When I told him that, he said, "Let me pray and ask the LORD to stop the hair from falling out." I tried to assure him that was not necessary, "No, that's alright." I really didn't want Bud to be disappointed when his prayer did not work. After all, everybody's hair falls out with radiation. Bud didn't press the issue. However, when we stopped to eat and bowed our heads to give thanks for the food, he slipped his hand onto my head and asked God to stop the hair from falling out. My thoughts were, "Oh no Bud, now you've done it. Now you are going to be so disappointed." Imagine how shocked I was when my hair stopped falling out! How was it possible that just because someone placed his hand on my head and prayed a short prayer, my hair stopped falling out? Yet, it was true. It actually began growing back while the radiation treatments continued.

I began to realize there was a lot more to know about God than I thought. He was beginning to reveal Himself to me as my healer. I knew Jesus was my Savior. And I even knew God could heal people. Still, was He actually healing me? I started to read Scripture concerning healing in a whole new way.

God healed me completely. Since that day, the doctors have not been able to find any cancer in my body. That was thirty-two years ago. When God heals, He does a good job. Praise His name.

Bud was a part of a coffee house style Bible study. Shirley and I began to attend. We learned many things about God and were actually beginning to know Him. We also started attending some Full Gospel Businessmen's meetings. I'll never forget the first time we saw somebody fall to the floor when someone prayed for him. [It is often referred to as 'being slain in the Spirit.'] It really frightened me, and yet I felt the presence of God in that meeting. Shirley told me she had many of the same concerns that I had. While attending a meeting like that we would get really high in spirit. Yet when we got home, or even on the way home, we would argue over something that was usually very minor. I couldn't understand why this would happen. I talked to Bud and Gertrude and they prayed with me that God would make Shirley and me one.

Then things got worse.

Chapter 5

TEARS OF JOY

On November 6, 1980, the Methodist church just down the street from where we were living at that time had a renewal meeting. I heard reports that great things were happening there. So, I said to Shirley, "Let's go!" She wasn't so sure, and besides the next day was our daughter's birthday, so Shirley stayed home. I went anyway and was not disappointed. The presence of God was surely in that place. I saw Larry Nofziger go forward to give his heart to the LORD. Larry was well known around town. He always talked to each person he met, laughing and joking with every one.

When I got home that night, I was so excited. I began telling Shirley about the meeting and then prophesied to her. I didn't know that it was called prophesying at the time, but what I said came to pass. I said, "This town will never be the same because Larry got saved tonight." It came true. Instead of joking with everyone, Larry was telling them about Jesus. Anyway, I was telling Shirley all about this when she suddenly started crying. I couldn't figure that out. LORD knows I had driven her to tears many times since my encounter with God. I had tried to force her to understand and step into this new life in the same way that I had. I felt so bad. It's just that I had been so excited to tell her about what happened down at the Methodist church. I apologized, "I'm sorry Honey. I don't want to make you cry."

Her response to me was something I had longed to hear for a year and a half. She said, "Don't ever say you are sorry. I want what you've got, but I don't know how to get it!" I nearly floated off the bed where we were talking. In fact, I think I could have walked on the ceiling. I said, "You can have it, all you need to do is ask." In that moment, the world seemed very quiet. I waited.... Finally, I said, "But you have to ask. I can't ask for you."

Again, there was silence for some time. All at once, she started praying, "LORD Jesus, come and fill me with your love." And He did! Our relationship began to change dramatically. I no longer felt that I was out there by myself. We seemed to be able to talk things out without getting upset with each other. No longer were our lives on a roller coaster of emotions. With this new unity in the Spirit, we were one in a way that we never had been before. Oh, we still had times of struggle and disagreement, but now we had Jesus in the mix.

I remember telling her that night that God would show her something new to confirm His presence with her. When I got home from work the next day, she said, "Tom, God showed me something new today." I was excited! I quickly asked, "What was it?" She said, "Every time I would try to sing today, I couldn't." I thought that was strange. She had been singing since she was about eight or nine years old with her sisters. They were known as the Klopfenstein Sisters. She was so young when they first sang in church that she had to stand on a stool so she could see over the podium. So how could it be that now she couldn't sing? Why would God do that? I asked, "What do you mean you couldn't sing?" Her response was, "Every time I tried to sing the old hymns and songs that I have sung for years, all I could do was cry!" The songs had suddenly taken on new and fresh meaning to her. God is so good!

Soon after that, our church had a winter Bible study. We took a class on the subject of evangelism. Our teacher was Spirit-filled, but I didn't know that. One evening as we studied the Bible, I became overwhelmed by the presence of the Holy Spirit and began to cry right there in the classroom with all of my peers watching. I wept so much that I remember seeing the tears drip on my open Bible. Our teacher seemed to understand what was happening. He laid his hand on me and asked the class to pray for me because God was doing something in me. When he did that, I slid down off my chair onto my knees and just wept and wept. While traveling home that night, Shirley said to me, "Tom, I made a new commitment to God tonight too. I will never stand in your way again." And she never has. We still talk about matters that come up, but I always have the assurance that she wants the will of God just as much as I do.

We began to get involved with more and more new friends. Together, we loved to study the Bible and talk about Jesus. The more we fellowshiped around the Word of God and prayed together, the bolder we got. We started experimenting in praying for one another. I remember one evening when we had friends over to the house. One of them had a lump on her neck.

Ron Rupp, the leader of the Bible study at the coffee house, laid his hand on the lump and began to pray. All at once, he said, "There it goes!" And, the lump was gone. We had actually witnessed a miracle of healing right there in our living room.

I continued to go to work at the hardware store, but my heart was no longer in it. I would rather be reading the Word or having Bible study with others. One day when I came home from work, I said to Shirley, "There has been a song going over and over in my head. It goes, '*It's real, it's real. O I know it's real. Praise God the doubts are settled and I know, I know it's real.*'" I asked her if she knew what the song was so we could look it up in a songbook. I wanted to know what the verses said. She said, "No, I don't know the title to that song. However, a song has been going over and over in my head too. She said her song started out, "*O how well I do remember how I doubted day by day. And I did not know for certain that my sins were washed away.*"

We got out some songbooks and started looking. To our shock, we found that both of our songs were actually the same. She had the verse, and I had the chorus. Isn't God good? I did not realize how the Holy Spirit was already at work making us one.

The song in its entirety says:

Verse (I)

> *O how well I do remember*
> *how I doubted day by day,*
> *For I did not know for certain*
> *That my sins were washed away.*
> *When the Spirit tried to tell me,*
> *I would not the truth receive,*
> *I endeavored to be happy,*
> *And to make myself believe.*

Chorus

> *But it's real, it's real,*
> *O I know it's real;*
> *Praise God the doubts are settled,*
> *For I know, I know it's real.*

Verse (2)

> When the truth came close and searching,
> All my joy would disappear,
> For I did not have the witness
> Of the Spirit bright and clear;
> If at times the coming judgment
> Would appear before my mind,
> O it made me so uneasy,
> For God's smile I did not find.

Verse (3)

> But at last I tired of living
> such a life of fear and doubt,
> For I wanted God to give me something
> I would know about;
> So the truth would make me happy,
> And the light would clearly shine,
> And the Spirit gave assurance
> That I'm His and He is mine.

Verse (4)

> So I prayed to God in earnest,
> And not caring what folks said;
> I was hungry for the blessing,
> My poor soul it must be fed;
> When at last by faith I touched Him,
> And, like sparks from smitten steel,
> Just so quick salvation reached me;
> O bless God I know it's real!

Written by H. L. Cox

I had another dream. I was in a big room where ministry was going on. I noticed this very large cross in the ceiling of the room. I awoke, but the dream puzzled me. [Pay attention to your dreams. God is trying to talk to you. The Bible tells of many times when God spoke to His people through dreams. For example, there was Joseph in the Old Testament, along with the butler and the baker. In the New Testament, there was another Joseph, the earthly father of Jesus, plus Peter, Paul, Elizabeth and others.]

Someone gave us a book titled *Following the Fire*, written by Gerald Derstine, a Mennonite who experienced a visitation of God back in 1955. "For seven days," he recounted, "We did not eat, sleep, or do anything except by the instruction of God."

I highly recommend the reading of this book if you are searching for the reality of God in your life. After I read this book, I learned about a school that Gerald called the School of the Spirit offered at Christian Retreat in Bradenton, Florida. I thought we should check it out.

A few months later, my family and I traveled to Florida for a vacation in a motor home I borrowed from my cousin. On the way, we picked up two hitchhikers, young boys who were going to Florida. We stopped from time to time to prepare a meal and invited the two boys to eat with us. I kept looking for an opportunity to tell them about Jesus. We were almost to the place in Florida where they wanted to get out when I saw my chance. After telling them that God loved them and had a wonderful plan for their lives, we were blessed to lead them to the LORD.

When we got to Florida, I decided to visit Christian Retreat, the location of Gerald Derstine's ministry. When we drove onto the grounds, we sensed the presence of the LORD. I remember how I just wanted to hug Shirley and all of my children. [Still today, the presence of the LORD permeates the atmosphere at Christian Retreat. You can actually feel it.]

We drove up to the main Tabernacle to go to a service. When we walked in, I began to tremble. This was the room I had seen in my dream with the huge cross in the ceiling made of lights! They put that cross up there as a constant reminder of the sign left in the ceiling of the little house in Minnesota at Strawberry Lake Christian Retreat. It 'appeared' in the ceiling there when God visited Gerald Derstine and the Mennonites in 1955. Could it be that God wanted me to attend this School of the Spirit? I was sure He did, but there was no way. How could I support my family for ten weeks without a job? I didn't have a big savings account. Nevertheless, I began to pray and the desire to go kept getting stronger.

We returned to Ohio and made plans to make the temporary move to Christian Retreat. I was reading in Psalm 24:3–5, "Who may ascend into the hill of the LORD? And who may stand in His holy place? He who has clean hands and a pure heart. Who has not lifted up his soul to falsehood. And has not sworn deceitfully. He shall receive a blessing from the LORD and righteousness from the God of his salvation"(NASB). I certainly wanted to be able to ascend into the hill of the LORD and stand in His holy place. However, God showed me that I had unclean hands and an impure heart.

Years earlier, when I had been a traveling sales representative for the Archbold Ladder Factory, they supplied the gasoline for my car. I would be sure to fill up the car on Friday afternoon so I would have a full tank for my own use on the weekend. I was stealing from my employer and therefore had unclean hands. I went to see my former boss at his home, confessed what I had done and offered to pay for the gasoline. He responded, "Tom, that was years ago. You owe nothing. I forgive you the debt."

What a relief! I left with a new freedom in my spirit. That lasted until God showed me where I had an impure heart. When I was managing the hardware store, I had an employee that I wanted to replace but did not tell the staff member my wishes. I simply refused to give a raise in pay hoping the employee would quit. I finally did receive the resignation. Now years later, God was urging me to go see this former worker and ask forgiveness. I knew I could not move forward in God if I did not obey.

I called this former staff member and asked if I could stop by the house. The employee said they had retired for the night and asked if I could come some other time. Since I was leaving early the next morning, I explained that I must discuss something before I left, so consent was given for me to come over. When I explained why I was there, the employee did admit that I had caused hurt by my actions. We had prayer together and our relationship was restored.

Shirley and I packed up our bags and borrowed money to buy a pop-up up camper. Christian Retreat has campgrounds making it less expensive to stay there than in the motel. A pop-up up camper in Florida for ten weeks, in the middle of the summer with four children and no air conditioner, is HOT! Nevertheless, off we went, as I once heard someone say, "Fat, dumb and happy." We had just embarked on a new and exciting journey. Little did we know what the future held in store for us.

Chapter 6

HOLY FIRE!

The Institute of Ministry (I.O.M.) is a ten-week intense school of the Spirit. It is not like a regular Bible school. It is not an academic school. The concept that God gave to Gerald was that of a can of concentrated orange juice. That juice in concentrated form would be bitter. However, when mixed with the right amount of water it becomes very sweet, delicious and nourishing. Gerald said, "If we pack the Word of God in concentrated form into human vessels and then send them back to their home church and to their job, when they mix with their fellowman that Word will become sweet, delicious and nourishing." That is the intent of the I.O.M.

I have said many times that the I.O.M. was the greatest ten weeks of my life. It was also the most trying ten weeks of my life. When we are being stretched, it is painful, but it enlarges our capacity to give out. And stretch us it did.

The first week our speaker was Henry Vanderbush from Marshall, Minnesota. He is known as the 'Barnyard Preacher.' He holds revival meetings in barns throughout the Upper Midwest. After he preached and began to pray for those who responded to the call, they started to fall to the floor. Although I had witnessed this before a few times, it was never like this. We went to the door so we could leave quickly if necessary. Yet, we were drawn to stay there and watch. That was just the beginning. I would sit there many times and just cry. At other times I would struggle with what I heard because it was so different from what I had been taught from little on up. It is difficult to change your way of thinking, but we must in order to conform to the Word of God. This is the true meaning of the word repentance. Romans 12:2 says, "Do not conform any longer to the pattern of this world, but be transformed by the renewing of your mind. Then you will be able to test and approve what God's will is—His good, pleasing and perfect will" (NIV).

After three or four weeks, Shirley and I were stretched almost to the breaking point. I didn't think she was changing fast enough. And she thought I should just leave her alone. I thought our marriage was in jeopardy. One day I told Shirley that we were going over to Gerald's house for counseling. She said, "No we aren't." Later, we went for a walk. I had taken hold of her hand and started to drag her to his house. I don't care how sweet and well-mannered my wife is, there are times when even I know I have gone over the line. That was one of them. We went home without the counseling.

Our next test came in the faith realm. We had been hearing testimonies from the I.O.M. speakers of how God had supernaturally provided food, money and other things for them. We were also reading through the Bible during the ten weeks. I came across the scripture in Ecclesiastes 5:4–5 that says, "When you make a vow to God, do not delay in fulfilling it. He has no pleasure in fools; fulfill your vow. It is better not to vow than to make a vow and not fulfill it"(NIV). The Holy Spirit reminded me of a vow I had made some eight or ten months earlier to give $25.00 a month for a countywide crusade back in Ohio. I looked in my checkbook and realized I was six months behind. Our balance was about $154.00. Being the man of faith and power that I was (ha ha),with Shirley's agreement, I wrote a check for $150.00. I sealed it in an envelope, put one of our last postage stamps on it, walked boldly to the mailbox and dropped it in.

Now we were positioned for a miracle. However, before that envelope hit the bottom of the box, the thought went through my mind, "You idiot! Now, how are you going to feed your family for the remainder of the school year?" [I didn't know it was probably a demonic spirit at that time. I thought it was just me.] Remember, we had four children who liked to eat. I knew our food was short and it was already a struggle to try to keep cool without air conditioning in that pop-up camper. "You know," I thought, "I think you are right!"

I immediately went back to our camper, opened up the cupboard and pulled out all of the food we had. I think this was on a Tuesday. We counted out the number of meals we could eat. We realized we could eat through Friday morning breakfast and then needed to go to town after our afternoon class to get groceries. Shirley and I had been fasting from our noon meal anyway, but the children needed to eat. We prayed and made out a grocery list of what we needed to get. In my mind, I planned to go to the grocery store, put all of the groceries on our list in the cart, go up to the cash register and wait. I envisioned that I would look for money on the floor or for someone to approach me and say, "Let me pay for your groceries."

Each day at noon, we would pray and try to believe. By Thursday night I broke! I cried out in prayer, "God, Your Word says that 'never have I seen the righteous forsaken, or Your seed out begging for bread.' Now, LORD, tomorrow I will need to start begging." I cried myself to sleep. How do you make yourself believe to the point that you can have perfect peace? Part of the answer is in the fact that I reminded God of His Word.

On Friday morning, we had run out of milk for the cereal. Shirley and I decided not to eat any breakfast. I poured cereal in the bowls for the children and poured water on it. Then I prayed. "LORD, I ask you to make this water taste like milk." Guess what? He didn't do it! Our boys didn't say anything. However, our daughter, April, said very quietly, "I would rather eat the cereal dry." Again, I cried. I took her bowl for myself and gave her another bowl of dry cereal. I thought it wasn't fair to make my children eat cereal with water on it unless I ate it too. And I sure wasn't going to throw it away!

Shirley and I went to class. At noon, we headed home again to pray. We told no one about our situation. On our way back to the afternoon class, Paul Powers, one of our classmates who also lived in the campground, walked with us. He said, "I have some groceries that I can't use. Could you use them?" I nonchalantly said I thought we could. Inside I was jumping up and down. After class, Shirley and I went to the altar to pray and thank God for His provision. I also reminded Him that we still had several weeks to go. While we were praying, an older woman in our class came up behind us, tapped us on the shoulder and said she wanted to see us over at the motel lobby when we finished praying. When we got up, we headed over to the motel. As we walked in the front door, I saw her writing a check in exchange for cash at the front desk. Somehow, I knew she was planning to give us some money. I had been taught by my Mennonite parents that I should not take charity. My dad always said, "You should work for a living and put money aside so you never need to ask for a hand out." I wanted to run out, but I had this need. What should I do?

This dear woman came over to us and gave us $50.00. It seemed like $5,000.00. We thanked her as sincerely as we knew how to do and headed for our pop-up. When we got there, we found two bags of food sitting on our table. As we took the items out of the bags, we checked them off our grocery list. Though there were a few extra things that were not on the list, it did not completely fill the list of groceries we needed. We headed to town to buy the items that were not in the bags and completely filled out our list. We even had a few dollars left, enough to buy some laundry powder to wash our clothes. I never thought about needing detergent, but Shirley had.

We had just seen a miracle of supernatural provision! We had other miracles too. One time we were in a service with an older woman seated directly behind us. The speaker shared about how God had supernaturally provided for him. This woman tapped Shirley on the shoulder and whispered to her, "God said to tell you that He will take care of your children." I had not realized that Shirley had concerns and was praying for our children.

The next day, when Shirley was working in the retreat's cafeteria, the same woman walked up to Shirley and handed her $100.00 explaining that God had also instructed her to do that too. The woman seemed delighted to obey.

Classes continued. As we approached the end of the school, I began to ask the LORD what I should do when we finished. One of the things students were assigned to do in the way of hands-on ministry was to spend some nights manning the prayer line phones. Early in the morning on one such occasion, I dozed off because there were no calls. In a short dream, I heard God call my name. "Tom!" The person I saw was my wife, Shirley. Instantly, I awoke. I asked the LORD what He was saying to me. He gave me the understanding that He was going to answer my prayer concerning what I was to do when the school ended, and He was going to do it through Shirley. That was an amazing idea to me since Shirley had never told me she had heard the audible voice of God.

About a week later on a Sunday morning, Arnie Smith, the I.O.M. Administrator, was making some announcements in the morning service. He explained that they were starting a Pastoral Training School that would encompass three additional ten-week quarters to follow the Institute of Ministry. Those additional weeks would mean a total of one year of school.

Suddenly Shirley looked at me with these big wide eyes and whispered, "Did you hear that?" I said, "What? What did he say?" "No, not Arnie," she replied, "God just spoke to me!" I immediately asked her, "What did He say?" Her response was, "I will tell you after church." I was totally exasperated. If she could tell me that God had just spoken to her, surely she should also tell me what He said. Oh no, I had to wait! I guess I still needed to learn more patience.

After church Shirley told me, "God said, "SELL YOUR HOUSE!" Then she said He also wanted us to find a larger place to live. In addition, we were supposed to enroll the children in school here in Florida while I was to go to the Pastoral Training School. This was a major thing, but for some strange reason I believed her. We talked with the administrator and he simply said, "Well, put the house on the market. If it sells, it was God, if not, it wasn't." We were sure that it was God. I called a realtor back in Ohio and told him, "Put the house on the market. If it does not sell by a certain date, schedule an auction. We are going to sell it."

One day a camper pulled into the space beside us and set up camp. The next day they came over and asked if I had any matches to light their stove. We did have two little boxes, so I gave one box to them. I said, "When you leave, if there are any left,would you please return them." They said they would. A couple of days later, as they prepared to pull out, they returned the box. I put the matches in our drawer. That evening when I got the matchbox out to light our stove there was a $20.00 bill tucked inside the box. Yeah, I cried again.

When school was over, I hitched a ride to southern Ohio with a fellow student and then hitch hiked the rest of the way to Archbold. I had always wanted to try hitch hiking. While I was gone, Shirley found a job, rented a house, moved in and enrolled the children in school.

I hitched my way to Holgate, Ohio, and was dropped off at the entrance to town. Holgate is about thirty-five miles from my parents' place in Archbold. I walked most of the way through town when I saw a pickup truck with a bumper sticker on it parked near the Post Office. It read, "Jesus is the Bridge Over Troubled Waters." The owner of the pickup had stopped to pick up his mail so I commented to him, "I like your bumper sticker." He thanked me, and I walked on. When he came out of the post office, he got in his pickup, drove ahead to where I was walking and asked, "Where are you headed?" I said, "To Napoleon, the next town north." He said, "Jump in. I'm going that way." I love how God provides! I hadn't even stuck out my thumb.

He asked me what I had been doing, so we talked about Jesus. That was all I needed to get started. When we got to Napoleon, he asked where I lived. I said, "Just let me out anywhere. I'm actually going to Archbold." My destination was another twenty-five miles beyond Napoleon. However, I didn't want to ask him to drive farther than his destination. He said, "I'll take you there." He drove me all the way to my parents' driveway. We sat there and talked for a while longer. When I started to get out, he reached into his wallet and gave me $20.00. "Here," he said, "You may need this." Things like that just blew me away.

My parents were glad to see me. We talked for quite a while. I told them of the miracle of provision we had witnessed at I.O.M. My dad said, "Why didn't you call me when you had no money?" I had to confess, "I did not have enough money to make a phone call." He countered, "You could have always written me a letter." I admitted that I didn't even have enough money for a stamp. "Well," he said, "You still could have called collect!" I suppose I could have, but I wanted to see how God was going to work. I am glad I waited.

I finished some painting on our house, got things ready for the auction and packed the rest of the furniture and personal items into a trailer for the trip back to Florida. We sold the house at auction. I wondered if it would bring enough to pay off the mortgage, yet I was confident that I could leave that in God's hands. I also sold many household items to lighten our load. Shirley reminds me every so often that I sold some things that I shouldn't have, for instance her Sunbeam mixer, the freezer and some of April's dolls. It brought enough to pay off the mortgage and everything we owed. I had $500.00 left, just enough for the first quarter of tuition for the Pastoral Training School (P.T.S.). I could hardly wait to get started.

My parents drove me back to Florida. On the way, I had over twenty hours to tell them everything that God had been doing in my life. I remember while we drove and talked, the tears ran down my cheeks as I marveled at the goodness of God. To think that He cared enough for me that He revealed Himself to me in all His glory. He actually thought that a farm boy from northwest Ohio could be useful to Him. My parents listened with great interest and though they really didn't have much to say, I believe they pondered these things in their hearts. I don't think they fully understood what had happened to me.

When we got there, it was almost time for the first quarter of P.T.S. to start. My parents stayed a couple of days and then returned to Ohio, leaving me with strict instructions to keep them informed of the progress.

Chapter 7

TEMPERING FIRE!

Shirley went to work. And I jumped head first into my studies at the P.T.S. The children started their school classes as well. We were on the journey.

There were eleven other students in the class. We were like the twelve disciples. We had our John, Peter, Andrew and probably all of the rest. We were just like a bunch of hungry puppies. We wanted to learn everything. Sometimes it seemed like our teachers tried to make us learn everything at once. We not only had all of our studies, but we also were required to be in the evening service, at least on Friday night. There was a different guest speaker every week because Gerald wanted us to observe different kinds of ministries. We were also assigned to assist the moderator in those evening services.

I remember when it was my turn. Barry Schoeder was the moderator. Just before the service, he asked me if I would lead worship. I wasn't prepared and had to say no. That troubled me. So, that night after the service, I took time to create a series of praise and worship songs. If he ever asked me to lead worship again, I would be ready. I kept it in my Bible and sure enough, later he did ask me again. That time I was prepared.

I love to sing. My family grew up singing, though never professionally or anything like that. We just liked to sing. Now some people still tell me I don't sing all that well, but that never bothers me or stops me. The Bible says to make a joyful noise unto the LORD, so I just open my mouth and 'let 'er rip.' I may not know how to sing that well, and I may not know what key the song is written in. Nevertheless, it didn't matter when I led worship because the musicians were so talented they found where I was and played the piano and other instruments right along with me. People said to me later, "I sure like it when you lead worship because you put your whole heart into it." That is the secret to perfect praise. Matthew 21:16b says, "Out of the mouth of babes and nursing infants you have perfected praise." Perfect praise is when, like a child, you praise Him from your heart.

Arnie Smith was the administrator of the P.T.S. in addition to his leadership in the Institute of Ministry. He taught us things like homiletics and hermeneutics. I had trouble even knowing how to say these words, let alone knowing what they meant. One of the things we had to do was to prepare a fifteen-minute sermon and deliver it in front of our fellow students while they critiqued us. Now that can be very intimidating. You are preaching along and you suddenly see several students write something on their notepad. Your mind wants to ask, "What did I just do?" However, you must keep on with your message. I found out that it doesn't matter whether you are in front of a classroom of your peers or in front of your own congregation, you can't let what the people do bother you while you are speaking. Just keep on preaching.

One of my sermons was an evangelistic message. Now I wasn't trying to get the other students saved, I was just practicing my preaching. I suddenly thought of a song I had learned by the Hopewell Quartet, so I sang it. It went something like this.

Last night as I lay sleeping,
This dream came to me.
I dreamed about the end of times,
About eternity.
I saw a million sinners,
Fall on their knees to pray.

The Savior sadly shook His head,
And this I heard Him say,
"Sorry, I never knew you.
Depart from Me forevermore.
Sorry, I never knew you.
Go and serve the one that you served before."

I thought the time had come when I must stand the trial.
I told the LORD that I had been a Christian all the while.
But through the Book He then looked
And sadly shook His head.

Then placed me over on His left,
And this is what He said,
"Sorry, I never knew you,
I find no record of your birth.
Sorry, I never knew you.

Go and serve the one you served while on earth."
There was my wife and children
I heard each one's voice.
They must have all been happy
It seems they did rejoice.

With robes of white around them,
And crowns upon their heads,
My little girl looked up at me,
And this is what she said,
"Daddy, we can't go with you
We must stay on this lovely shore.
Sorry, for we still love you,
But you cannot be our Daddy anymore."

When I from sleep awakened,
With tears in my eyes,
I looked around
And there about me
To my great surprise.
I saw my wife and babies
And knew I'd had a dream.
Then down beside my bed I fell,
And for mercy did scream.

Father, who art in Glory
In mercy look on me today.
Forgive me, let me serve Thee.
Til the summons comes that calls me away.

Written by Sherman Branch

I could hardly make it through the song for the tears running down my cheeks and the choking in my voice, but it seemed like I had to sing that song. I now recognize that is what the anointing will do for you. When I finished, I noticed that others were crying also. They had obviously been touched by His hand as well. Now when that happens, I don't try to stifle it. I just go with it.

Still today, songs or poems from my distant past come to me when I am preaching. I have learned that God uses them to speak something intimate to someone out there, so I just go ahead and sing or quote it.

[Maybe that is you right now. If you sense His presence, if your heart is pounding, if there are tears in your eyes, perhaps He is calling you. Would you take a moment right now to talk to Him? He loves you and wants to set you free from any and all bondage and to take you on a journey with Him. I can assure you, He will never disappoint you. He will never leave you nor forsake you. Maybe you don't even know how to pray. Just say aloud right now,

> "Dear Jesus, have mercy on me. I confess You are Lord. I believe You have risen from the dead, are seated at the right hand of the Father and are praying for me right now. Take me and mold me into the vessel that You desire for me. I will follow You wherever You lead me. Thank you, Lord. Amen."

If you prayed that prayer, tell someone. Write to me and tell me. My contact information is at the back of this book. It is important that you speak out of your mouth and tell someone. It will strengthen you. Get into a Bible believing church and launch out on your journey with Him.]

As one of the students, I was assigned to preach at a local church as part of our training. I don't know how Arnie Smith found pastors willing to let us do that, but he did. We usually took several other students with us when we went. I remember one church where I preached. I got to this little church where I think the only ones that showed up were my fellow students, the pastor, his wife and the drummer with his bass drum. I had a severe headache but did not let that stop me. This was in a black culture church. The drummer began to beat on his drum and the pastor began to chant and rock back and forth entering into worship. I joined in with it. When it was time for me to preach, my headache was gone. God healed me during worship and the only instrument we had to accompany us was a big bass drum. How awesome is our God!

Praise and worship are very powerful ways to experience God's miracle working power. Many people are healed in His presence as they give themselves to Him in worship.

One of my favorite teachers was Floy Cox. He was raised a Baptist. In fact, he told us that he used to say, "I was Baptist born and Baptist bred, and when I die, I will be Baptist dead." Of course, after he received the Baptism of the Holy Spirit, he was no longer your normal Baptist preacher. He was teaching one day and the subject of casting out demons came up. He instructed us about how Jesus cast out demons with a word. He gave many illustrations of experiences he had in this kind of ministry.

A short time later, a ministry called Visible Light came to the retreat on a Saturday night. It employed technology that allowed slide pictures to fade and merge into what almost looked like a movie. There also was narration with it.

After the service, we had a habit of going over to the snack bar. When we walked out the back of the Tabernacle, I noticed a young man talking loudly with Phil Derstine, Gerald and Beulah's son. I told Shirley and the children to go in and get something to eat and I walked over behind the garbage can to where they were. I found out later that the young man had apparently been drinking or smoking some dope. He was angry because his girlfriend was working at the snack bar. It looked like there was about to be a fight. Phil had taken some karate lessons and jumped back into a karate stance. I was just standing nearby, praying in the Spirit under my breath. Suddenly my body began to vibrate. I found myself jumping between Phil and this young man.

I don't know what happened to Phil after that. My attention was totally focused on the situation I was facing. I pointed my finger at the young man and said, "I rebuke you in the name of Jesus!" He flew backward as if I had hit him with a baseball bat. He hit a car parked behind him and crumpled to the ground on his back. The next thing I knew, I was sitting on top of him with my hands on his chest pleading the blood of Jesus. He became very quiet, so I stood up. Everything seemed all right for a moment. Suddenly he coiled around my leg like a snake and bit me on the calf of my leg. It didn't hurt right then so I rather calmly said, "He is biting me." Again, I laid my hands on him and began to pray. It seemed like I was unable to cast out this second demon.

Suddenly I heard my fellow student, Gil Winn, come out of his nearby motor home. He was praying in the Spirit so loudly it sounded to me like a roar. He slowly walked over to see what was going on. I called out to him, "Agree with me in prayer." I reached up my hand, and the moment he took hold of my hand, the demon spirit came out, confirming the scripture that Jesus sent them out two by two. There is multiplied power in agreement. (See Mt 18:19, Lev 26:8.)

There was a friend of the young man standing there observing all of this. I went over to him and said, "Are you tired of living like this?" He said, "Yes." Right there I led him to Jesus and began to explain the scriptures to him. He asked, "Can I be baptized?" "Sure, come on," I answered. We went straight over to the swimming pool where I baptized him that same night.

When I got home, Shirley had already put the children to bed. When I opened the door still dripping wet, she looked a little surprised, so I had to explain.

God continued to guide us as we prepared for what He had ahead for us.

One night I had another dream. In the dream, I saw my administrator, Arnie. He told me that some of the staff people were talking about needing to add another ministry employee. Then he said, "I want you to be on staff here at Christian Retreat." It was Arnie's face that I saw, but it was God's voice that I heard. My response was, "I think that is wonderful, but you will have to tell Gerald because I won't." When I awoke, I told Shirley about the dream. She was as excited about it as I was. I thought about that dream often over the next weeks. I waited. You might say I pondered it in my heart.

One day when Gerald was teaching in the class, he suddenly looked at me and seemed to stop as if he was going to say something to me. After a short hesitation, he continued teaching. When he finished for the day, he asked to talk to me. He asked Shirley and me to go with him Sunday afternoon to help serve communion at Sun City Center, about one-half hour north of the retreat. Gerald had been conducting a Bible study with a group of people who wanted to start a church there. I could hardly wait to get home. When I saw Shirley, I told her what Gerald had requested. Then I asked her, "Do you suppose this is when he is going to ask me to be on staff?"

I thought Sunday would never come... but it finally did. After the morning service, Shirley and I got into the car with Gerald and Beulah. We drove to Ruskin where there was a little restaurant called the Coffee Cup that served up some great pies. We ordered lunch and talked while we waited for our food. Gerald seemed to be fidgeting with his silverware as if he was trying to think of what he wanted to say. I knew what was coming. Finally he said, "Several of us have been talking and your name came up. We would like to ask you to stay on after you have graduated from the P.T.S. and join the staff." When he finished, he lifted his eyes to look directly at me. I felt like I was grinning from ear to ear. He quickly added, "You may want to pray about it before you answer." I said, "Uh, sure. But I think I already know that my answer is yes."

We had been living about a half mile down the road from the retreat on Hagle Park Road. We began to look for a place to stay on the grounds of the retreat. We rented mobile home number ten. On Friday evening, my parents and my sister, Karen, and her husband, Lynn Rupp, came down from Ohio for my graduation. Then on Sunday, they were there for my ordination. The following Monday, I was on staff.

Chapter 8

WHAT A RIDE!

Gerald told me that I would be teaching in the I.O.M. Even though I had just finished this school myself, I was to teach already! This was just the beginning of a supernatural journey that would challenge me beyond anything I had ever experienced. I was assigned to teach Family Relationships. I enjoyed the work very much and got to know many students from all over the world.

I went walking early one morning during week seven or eight of that first I.O.M. in which I was teaching. Gerald approached me riding on his golf cart. He stopped and greeted me cheerfully. He told me, "I would like to have you become the administrator of the I.O.M. school for the next term." I was totally shocked! I didn't think I could handle that.

What I said was, "Gerald, administration is not my primary gift." I had been studying on the gifts of the Spirit and had them all in three neat categories: Ministry Gifts, Manifestation Gifts and Motivational Gifts. "However," I went on to say, "I will do anything you ask me to do to the best of my ability." He countered with, "Well, it will be just temporary." Actually, it continued for nearly four years.

There was about a two-week break between the end of one I.O.M. and the beginning of the next course. That gave me plenty of time to be completely organized. Ha! Thank God for good secretaries. Marge Peterson was the absolute best. She was able to keep me going in the right direction and made me look good. The position was challenging enough all by itself. However, it was even more intimidating to be the administrator and to have the former administrator as one of the teachers. Yet I was so busy, I didn't have much time to think about it.

I had just started when Gerald informed me that my job also included coordinating the correspondence school. A few days later, he told me that he also wanted me to take care of the Video I.O.M. and the Pastoral Training School. I felt like I had a tiger by the tail and didn't know how to let go. Neither did I want to let go.

My day started at 6:00 a.m. with early morning prayer that ended at 7:00. Breakfast was served from 7:00 to 7:30, followed by a staff chapel meeting from 7:30 to 8:00. The first class was from 8:00 to 9:00, break from 9:00 to 9:15 and the second class was from 9:15 to 10:15. There was another fifteen-minute break and an hour-and-a-half session with the main conference speaker. Lunch followed, plus another one-hour session of class in the afternoon. We then had a break until 7:00 in the evening when we would again be in the service. These sessions were rarely over before 10:00 or 10:30 at night. That was my schedule each day, Tuesday through Friday. On Saturdays, we quit early and didn't have an afternoon class. Of course, on Sunday we had two services as well. Monday was our day off. I calculated that the students attended as much in ten weeks as most people do in five years. That is what I call packing it in, in concentrated form.

Opening day of my first school term came. We had registration and orientation. Then I assigned seats to the students and we were off. I taught about three to four classes each week, coordinated the other local teachers and the outside speaker for the week. We also had a different conference speaker ministering to the students each week in the mornings and evenings.

In each school, Gerald Derstine would have one session where he would share his testimony of the visitation of God he and his family had experienced back in 1955. That was always a highlight of the school. I would sit in and listen each time. There were a few times when he was unable to give that testimony live, so we had it video recorded to be sure that each class would be able to experience it. I remember during one of those video presentations, while watching from the balcony, I noticed some of the students sleeping. Tears came to my eyes because I could not understand how anyone would waste such an incredible opportunity.

Gerald, of course, always taught on the subject of the Kingdom of God. I don't think it matters how often I hear those messages, I still continue to get more revelation each time I hear them. [I will get to more of that later.]

I was the administrator for only a short time when Gerald and Floy Cox went to Israel with a tour group. It seemed like I was left behind and was the only other person remaining in the ministry department. How did this farm boy from northwest Ohio come to be in this place? Gospel Crusade Inc., the parent ministry of Christian Retreat, is a worldwide ministry operating retreat centers, a Bible school, Pastoral Training School, mission works and so much more. With both Gerald and Floy gone, I sensed I had the whole thing placed on my shoulders. It felt like I was in way over my head. Thank God, there wasn't any major crisis and they returned soon.

During one of the schools, we had two women arrive late, after the school had already started. "God told us we had to come to this school," they said. Now I was pretty green and thought, "Well if God told you to come, who am I to say you have to wait until the next school?" I enrolled them and they started coming to classes. I was about to learn something. They were so 'spiritual,' giving utterances in tongues and prophecies over other students.

The I.O.M. policy stated that when a student came to the school for the ten-week course, they were to lay aside whatever ministry they had been doing so they could give themselves to learning and hearing from God. I spoke to the two women several times about this. They would listen but continued to break the policy. I became more and more uncomfortable about it. I had other students come to me and tell me that they were also very uncomfortable with these two women. I was praying regarding what to do. Some students later told me they also were praying that someone would do something. It troubled me for many days, sort of like the situation Paul experienced with a woman, possessed by a spirit of divination, who prophesied over his apostolic team.

> *She kept this up for many days. Finally, Paul became so* <u>*troubled*</u> *that he turned around and said to the spirit, "In the name of Jesus Christ I command you to come out of her!" At that moment, the spirit left her.* [Emphasis mine.]   (Acts 16:18, NIV)

One Sunday these two women were in the morning service. I was moderating and Floy Cox was to speak. Tom Gill was leading worship. We reached an awesome high place in worship. The Presence of the LORD was unusually strong. A song had just ended and we were basking in His glorious presence. Suddenly, one of these women began shrieking loudly. I immediately sensed the presence of the LORD begin to lift. Then she was silent.

Tom Gill realized what had happened and began singing another song of worship. Very gently, the Holy Spirit began to descend again. The Spirit can be resisted and His strong presence will diminish. I asked Floy, "If she does that again, should I rebuke her?"

Floy said very emphatically, "YES!" Tom Gill led us back into that special place with God once again. You guessed it. She began shrieking again. I put my hands on my knees to stand up and the next thing I remember, I saw my right foot as it landed on the armrest on the front row of seats. Others that saw me go said I shot off the stage. The woman was in the third row. I jumped over the front row and into the second row, laid my hand on her head and said to the demon, "I command you in the name of Jesus to come out of her." (See Acts 16:18.) After the demon had been cast out, she continued to mutter, "No Tom. You're wrong. You're wrong." I heard myself command her, "If you don't shut up, we will carry you out of this service!"

Suddenly I felt as weak as a newborn kitten. Every bit of strength or virtue had been sucked completely out of me. I painstakingly crawled back over the seats and stumbled to the stage. I literally crept back to my seat on my hands and knees, knelt at the chair and began to pray fervently. "Dear God, please come back and manifest Your presence to the people one more time." There is nothing like the presence of the LORD and I did not want Him to leave. He responded and blessed us once again with His awesome, glorious presence.

We discovered later that the two women were out of proper relationship with their husbands. Moreover, they had disrupted services back in the church where they were from. When they insisted that God had told them they were to be in that particular school, I should have realized that if God had indeed told them to come, then He should have known when the school started. I was beginning to learn, but painfully slow.

I had to dismiss them from the school. We survived. In fact, God blessed the school tremendously. Prior to this, I never thought I could kick someone out of Bible school, but I did. I needed this lesson for other challenges looming on the horizon.

In one school, Ken Sumrall was scheduled to be the first conference speaker. He had been in the Charismatic Movement from the early days, and was highly respected for his balanced ministry. He wrote a book titled *Organized Flexibility*. Ken became sick and had to cancel just a short time before his scheduled week. A staff member quickly invited a friend of his to fill in, along with his family. He told me that they 'just happened' to have that week available on their calendar.

This ministry family was totally unknown to me, but I had plenty of other things to do, so I went along with the staff member's suggestion. When they started to minister I was so disappointed, partly because it wasn't Ken Sumrall and partly because I did not agree with their style of ministry. I would hear them call out a sickness or disease for a particular person that didn't know anything about having such a sickness. Then they would pray for that individual and announce a total healing. That bothered me as well as some other theological things they said. I thought, "What will happen to these students who were expecting Ken Sumrall and hear this. Will they leave the school?"

I expressed my concerns to Gerald's secretary. She said she would speak to Gerald about the matter. At that time, Gerald was at the Strawberry Lake Christian Retreat in Minnesota. When I returned to her office late that day she said, "Gerald said if you are uncomfortable with the ministry let them go and have Floy finish the week." I literally fell on my knees, overwhelmed with the responsibility that had just been given me from Gerald. I immediately went to speak with Floy Cox. He agreed with me and said I should give the ministry the same honorarium they would have received if they had completed the whole week. After all, they were in full-time ministry and depended on offerings for their livelihood. Then Floy left to go home and prepared for the evening service.

I did not make this decision lightly. In fact, it was the most difficult decision I had ever made. It was necessary to dismiss a few students from Bible school, but this was a far different story. I had the accounting department cut a check. I took the check in my hand and went to see the leader of this ministry. As I walked down the hall of the Miracle Manor motel toward the speaker's suite, I thought, "I must take care of the business entrusted to me for the sake of the I.O.M. and the students sent here by God for instruction." Not one of the students ever knew what took place.

I knocked on the door of their room. When they opened the door, I went in to deliver the message and the honorarium. They did not agree with me, however, my decision was made. I respectfully explained that their services would not be needed for the remainder of the week. They informed me that they had cancelled meetings to fill in at Christian Retreat. That was not the story I had been told when they were invited. Remember, I had been told that it just so happened that they had that week open.

The next day, as they were leaving the retreat grounds, they made a special effort to come by my office to speak to me. They explained that they needed to warn me that I would not be in the ministry for long. I felt they were saying that I would die soon. I countered, "I do not receive those words." I excused them and went back to work.

Chapter 9

THE ANGELIC AND THE DEMONIC

I have learned that God doesn't wait for us to become perfect before He begins to lead us into ministry or even to a ministry school. He is looking for people who have a perfect heart toward Him—people He can mold, change and lead far beyond anything they ever dreamed possible. One such person is Jim Lumberson.

When Jim Lumberson and his wife, Shari, came to the I.O.M., I saw a man and a family who desired to do God's will, whatever the cost. They gave themselves to following God fully. When they finished the I.O.M., Jim immediately enrolled in the Pastoral Training School. When things from our past try to derail God's plan for us, He graciously cleans them out in His perfect timing. When this begins to happen, it will usually seem like it is a bad thing. But trust me, it is not. Romans 8:28 tells us, "And we know that all things work together for good to those who love God, to those who are the called according to His purpose."

One Friday, Shari called me and said, "Jim has been arrested. And I don't know where they have taken him!" I immediately thought, "What in the world is going on now?"

I began a search, starting at the sheriff's office and the jail... no answers. I knew a deputy personally, so I called him to see if he could find out anything. The only answer was, "You will need to wait until Monday when the offices are open." On Monday, I found out they had transported Jim to Tampa. So, off I went with a student from Tampa who knew something about the way the authorities worked. First, we went to the La Teresita restaurant to look for Louis CapDevilla, another student [and another story that will follow]. He had a firsthand understanding of where to look. When we walked into the restaurant and asked for Louis, we got some pretty strange looks. They wouldn't tell me a thing. I guess they thought I was a narc or something.

We finally ended up at the Tampa jail. I identified myself as a pastor and asked to see Jim. They put me in a room and told me to wait. Finally, Jim came into the room. He told me later that I was the first friendly face he had seen since being arrested three days earlier.

The local newspaper came out with headlines that read, "Minister Arrested at Christian Retreat."

Here is Jim's testimony in his own words:

....

"I served the devil for forty-six years and hated and persecuted Christians. I was an agnostic and believed in Darwin's theory of evolution. My father was a member of the Klu Klux Klan and a maker of bathtub gin during the prohibition. I can't remember him ever saying, "I love you." My mother was a psychic, believed in the occult, levitation and reincarnation. She practiced spiritualism on a daily basis.

I never entered a church. I never saw a Bible and no one ever told me there was a God who loved me. I purposely ran away from home many times as a young child. My father finally put a dog collar on me and chained me to a clothesline. I was raised in the poorest neighborhood in town and was ashamed to bring my friends to my home.

At seventeen years of age, I joined the Navy to get away. After my discharge, I played college football. During my freshman year, I invented a device for N.A.S.A. that was placed in the Apollo and Gemini command modules. I became a multimillionaire and lived in a thirty-five room mansion in Miami. I had a private plane, a yacht, maids and butlers. I was attracted to and associated with only the intellectuals and the wealthy jet setters.

Although I had all that the world said was important, I was really bored and life was not exciting enough. Through my Italian heritage and political contacts, I began to arrange connections between the Columbian cartels and drug dealers in the United States. I was introduced to cocaine by two so-called friends, a medical doctor and a criminal court judge. When I thought I was at the top of the mountain by the world's standards, I was really in the pit of Hell.

There was a void in my life, but I didn't know what it was. The devil had my soul and I was tormented daily. Then, as I was reaching the 'end of my rope,' I met Shari in 1980. I had been dating her younger sister. Shari was the first Christian woman I had ever known. She let me know early on that she was not interested in dating me if I continued in my existing lifestyle.

I reluctantly moved from Miami, bought a large R.V. and we travelled around the country getting to know each other, much to the chagrin of her parents. We returned to Winter Haven and were married.

Shari became pregnant and our first baby, Lindsey Ann Lumberson, was born in 1982. She had a congenital heart problem. She was transported by ambulance to Shands Teaching Hospital in Gainesville, Florida. When she was three days old, at 2:00 in the morning of the fourth day, I went to the hospital chapel. Since I did not know how to pray, I tried to make a deal with a God that I did not know.

I said, "Take my life not hers, because everything I have ever done has been selfish. Let my baby live." I did not believe that God heard that prayer so I went on, "I will give this baby to You God. And if You can use me just as I am, I will serve you the rest of my life."

Instantly, all of the sins I had ever committed were lifted and removed; I was saved, healed and delivered. I returned to the baby's room and picked her up. She opened her eyes, squeezed my hand and seemed to say, "Daddy, everything is going to be all right now that you've accepted Jesus."

A few hours later, she died on the operating table. God gave me strength to minister to my wife and family. At the graveside the preacher said, "God used this angel to bring her daddy to Christ." Several people were saved that day.

Six weeks later, I was enrolled in Bible College. I thought that God had 'given me a pass' since I was a Christian now. One year later, in 1983, I was arrested for the terrible things I had been involved in during the 1960s and 1970s. I was initially expecting to be sentenced to life plus twenty-five years, with no possibility of parole, through the RICO statute. However, God performed a miracle and the judge said he did not believe I was a career criminal like the others who were arrested with me. He withheld adjudication and sentenced me to five years of probation. That was twenty-seven years ago. The Christian community accepted me.

Every demon on earth and in Hell trembles when I share my testimony because I now stand as a radical example of God's grace, His redemption and His restoration. No matter what challenges you may be facing today, you can and will be used by God if you will just surrender your heart to Him. To God be all the glory, worship and praise." [Posted here with Jim's permission.]

....

Louis CapDevilla, the fellow student mentioned earlier, is another example of God's marvelous grace. Louis was born in Havana, Cuba, in 1957. At the age of five years old, he immigrated to Tampa, Florida, with his family.

I will pick up his story in his own words:

....

"I was born fat, ugly and poor. Some are born fat, but not ugly. Others are born ugly, but not poor. Still others are born poor, but not fat. I was born with all three, and I hated myself. My journey to find out why I was born this way started early in my life. Why was I born in these conditions when so many had it all?

To make matters worse, I was forced to work selling hot tamales at the age of seven with my big brother who was nine. It was not that we did not want to work and help my parents, but there were days when we did not want to go out and sell tamales, yet we had to. At the age of ten, while all my friends were enjoying their three-month school vacation break, I was working hard at my Uncle Juan's meat market on the weekends. At fifteen, my parents bought a small grocery store that became a supermarket. My brothers and I were part of the work team. I had heard through my grandmother that the reason we had to work was because Adam's sin made work mandatory. I always said within myself that when I got to heaven I was going to visit Adam and give him a tongue-lashing.

I remember that finally at sixteen I lost weight, grew an afro hairdo and put on these big high heel shoes. The results were that I became a popular guy and everyone wanted to hang out with me. At the height of my popularity, surrounded by loads of friends, I still hated myself. I did not like who I was, and my self-esteem was on the floor. I constantly had to be someone I was not, instead of being myself.

This state of mind caused me to continue to search for truth. If God really did exist, where was He and why did He allow suffering and the innocent to die? Unfortunately, I turned to a life of drugs and drug dealing. I continued to question God and even wrote letters to God. In the latter part of this chapter of my life, I would read my Bible between drug deals.

Besides running drugs, I also stole money from mob members. They kept their money in their basements and attics. I would often disable the security systems before invading their home. The only time I got busted was when I went after two million dollars.

God was dealing with me for many years before I finally submitted my life to Him. I went on a ten-day trip to New York City to party down. I took along ten thousand dollars and a pound of cocaine. New York City is one of those places that you can party twenty-four hours a day in its hundreds of clubs and hot spots. I hooked up with two ex-felons who just recently had been released from jail. We partied for what seemed like days. When we could not party anymore, we went back to my hotel to get some rest. I immediately sat on the bed with the intention of going to sleep. Suddenly I heard this voice that said in a stern loud voice, "If you fall asleep you will die!" The voice was so real. I instantly told one of my friends to go get some food. When he left, I told the other friend to go get me some cigarettes. As soon as they were both gone I scurried around packing clothes and got out of there fast. I knew these guys were planning to kill me.

Now I know that the voice I had heard was the voice of the Holy Spirit. While I was yet a sinner, God was with me and calling me.

There was another time when I was in a Ramada Inn and I was desperate. My life was a wreck and I was contemplating suicide. There was a Bible and a gun laying on the bed when I finally cried out to God for help. Out of nowhere, I heard a voice that said, "Go to church." The voice was so real. I got in my car and drove to the only church I knew, my local Catholic church where I only attended on Christmas and Easter. It was very dark at three in the morning. When I attempted to open the door, I was shocked and anger began to burn within me. I screamed to myself, "Why would they lock the doors to the church if God lives there?" I turned to leave but that voice spoke once again, "Pull both doors!" I whirled around and put both of my hands on the doors. To my amazement, they opened. I made my way through the thick blackness and found a seat. I fell into the pew and exploded in great sobs and wails as I cried out to God.

It must have been about fifteen minutes later when I heard the door behind me open. Someone tapped me on the shoulder, put a flashlight in my face and growled, "What are you doing here?" I shot back, "What do you think I am doing? I need help!" It was the cops! They took me outside and frisked me. Then they started grilling me. Finally, they found the priest and explained that I needed help.

Would you believe it? The priest barked out emphatically that if I did not get off the property he would have me arrested. I had come to the church empty and crying out to God and this is how I was being treated. It angered me to the point that I snapped out of my depression.

The mob got tired of me stealing from them and put a contract out on my life. I had stolen money and drugs from this guy who had been a good friend of mine. However, in my desperation, I had crossed him and he was furious. I got out of town and headed back to New York City to hide out. Several weeks went by and I was tired of hiding out. I placed a call to a friend of mine in Tampa, Florida, where my family was living. I asked him to mediate with the mob on my behalf so I could come home.

Two days later, I received a response, a green light to return. However, there were certain payback conditions attached.

I arrived home on a Wednesday evening. Someone invited me to go to church on Sunday evening. For the first time in my life, I went to a Bible preaching church with my heart open to receive. There was an Italian missionary preaching who spoke of three things that radically changed my life. "First," he proclaimed, "If you come to Christ, He will forgive you of all your sin." When I heard that I knew that was exactly what I needed if I was to get a fresh start. "Next," he went on, "If you come to Christ He will give you power to change." I immediately thought of how many times I had told my dad that I was truly going to change, only to find out when nighttime came, I went back to the same old temptations. "The third thing," the preacher continued, "If you come to Christ, He will give you eternal life!" My heart leaped. When you break into mobsters' homes, steal drugs and money from them and then carry those drugs through airports, you are constantly staring death in the face.

That Easter Sunday, I gave my life to the LORD and was born again. My mom took one look at my face when I got home and exclaimed, "What happened to you?" Apparently, she could see the change.

I sent a message to the mobster that I would not be returning his money to him because it was drug money. Instead, I was going to give it all away. They came to our family restaurant twice and threatened to kill me right in front of my father. I simply raised my hands to heaven and told them I was not running. I was not afraid to die because I now had Jesus in my life. They left!

One month later the mobster died in a plane crash returning from a big cockfight in Miami. I was no longer continuously pursued. That chapter of my life was over. I threw myself totally into service for the LORD. During the next two years, all I did was go to work, go to church and study my Bible at home.

I enrolled in the Institute of Ministry at Christian Retreat and have never looked back." [Edited and posted here with Louis' permission.]

....

Since Louis graduated from the Institute of Ministry, he has planted over 250 churches, mostly in other nations. I tell of these two students to show how God's grace can take some of the worst and change them. And He can do the same for you!

One day I received a phone call stating that Sarah, one of the residents in a duplex on the retreat grounds, was in trouble and needed help right away. I got on my golf cart and went to her house. The front door was locked. A neighbor told me her son was holding her hostage. I knew her son so I went around to the back door, knocked and let myself in. Her son Bill was in the kitchen near the front door. Sarah started to explain that her son became angry with her and would not let her out of the house. Bill had injured himself when he jumped from a train car after he had hitched a ride. Because of that, he had acquired some medical problems.

I tried to talk calmly to Bill and said, "Bill, you don't want to do this." As he turned his attention toward me, his mother got up from the sofa and went out the front door. Thank God, she was safe now. He then reached into a kitchen drawer and pulled out a BIG BUTCHER KNIFE. As he started walking toward me, I blurted out, "I bind every evil spirit in Jesus' name."

He kept coming. Again, I stated a little more emphatically, "I bind every evil spirit in Jesus' name." He mocked me and just kept coming. By this time, he had come within two feet in front of me. I had the realization that my hands seemed to be so heavy, they just hung at my side. He said, "I will spill your guts out with this knife!" as he took a swipe at my midsection. It seemed like there was an invisible shield in front of me and he could not penetrate it.

In a flash, my mind saw headlines in the paper, "Preacher's Guts Spilled on Floor by Man with Butcher Knife." I thought about my wife, Shirley, and was saddened at the thought of her being left alone. "If I am going to die like this, I will at least try one more time," I thought. So once more, I said boldly, "I bind every evil spirit in Jesus' name!" Bill just mocked me again. He hit me in the throat with the hand that did not have the knife in it. I fell against the back door of the house, but it was latched. As he yelled for me to get out of his house, he reached around behind me and opened the door, which allowed me to go out. I was supernaturally calm throughout this whole ordeal.

I went around to the front of the house, got on my golf cart and drove over to Gerald's home. The further I went, the more I began to tremble. By the time I reached his house, I was a mess. When Gerald came out, I tried to tell him what had happened. I was so weak I could hardly stand up. Gerald spoke calmly and prayed for me. That calmed me immensely.

Someone called 911. We learned later that Bill had not taken his medication. The medics took him to the hospital but he was soon able to return to his home. He came to me several times and apologized. His favorite song was "I Come to the Garden Alone." Bill always liked the luminaries that we would put out as decorations at Christmas time.

I had the privilege of sharing at Sarah's home going funeral service and I remember quoting from Matthew 5:16, "Let your light so shine before men, that they may see your good works and glorify your Father in heaven." I changed the word light to luminary. Bill really appreciated that.

Every Saturday evening we held a concert at Christian Retreat. We had every genre of music you can imagine, from contemporary to Southern Gospel and everything in between. On one occasion when the Blackwood Brothers were singing, there was a young man there from Fort Meyers, Florida.

I noticed that he looked ill and his hair was very thin. He left the tabernacle during the concert. I was concerned for him, so I followed him out. He explained, "I have Crohn's disease and it is very painful." I had never heard of Crohn's disease, but I asked him if I could pray for him. He agreed, so I simply just prayed for his healing in Jesus' name. He stayed outside and I went back in.

About six months later, he came again. When he saw me, he hustled over to me and asked if I remembered him. I honestly did not. He looked very healthy and had a nice head of hair. He reminded me, "You prayed for me at a concert about six months ago, don't you remember?" Then I remembered. He pulled out a newspaper clipping and showed it to me. The headline read, "Man Healed of Crohn's Disease." The article explained that there is no cure for Crohn's disease but went on to document his healing. I was amazed. When you pray for people, you may not know whether they receive their healing or not. However, that's okay. That is God's business. Paul Powers, a friend from my I.O.M. class would often say, "I just want to do the people stuff and let God do the God stuff."

My responsibilities included scheduling the prayer partners on the twenty-four hour prayer line. One night at 2:00 or 3:00 in the morning, my phone rang. It was the phone counselor stating that someone was at the door knocking and requesting to be let in. Phone counselors were instructed not to let anyone in, especially at night. I pulled some clothes on, jumped on my golf cart and hurried over to the prayer line mobile home.

When I arrived, I noticed a car with a wheel chair strapped to the trunk. I also saw two men. One was standing near the mobile home that housed the prayer phones. The other man was in the driver's seat of the car. I asked the man who was standing outside what I could do for them. He explained that he had met the driver at a Seven-Eleven convenience store. The man was looking for a place to sleep. He said, "I told him that if he would go to Christian Retreat he would get some help. He didn't know the way, so I rode out here with him." From my conversation with this man, I understood the man in the car was 'broke, busted and disgusted.'

I asked this man what his name was. He said, "That's not important." I insisted, "What is your name?" He finally told me something that I couldn't remember the moment after he said it. However, it satisfied me for the time being.

We went over to the car. I reached my hand through the open driver's window, laid my hand on the man's shoulder and said, "Let's pray." The other man was standing right next to me on my left. I prayed a very short prayer. As I was praying I heard the man on my left shuffle his feet on the gravel. When I said, "Amen," I lifted my eyes and this man on my left was GONE! I mean GONE. I looked up and down the street. I walked all the way around the mobile home. He was nowhere to be found. Looking back, I am sure that he was an angel.

I returned to the man in the car and asked what I could do for him. He said that he was just so tired and needed a place to sleep. He told me that he used to sing Gospel music with his family. They had traveled in ministry for some time. He had suffered a stroke that left him paralyzed on his left side. Having compassion for him, I took him over to the motel and got a key to a room for him. I put him in a room for the night and went home to get some sleep.

The next morning, when this man came out of the motel in his wheel chair, I observed several retreat staff and residents stop and pray for him. I arranged for him to have some breakfast. Then he got in his specially equipped car and drove off. I didn't expect to hear from him again.

Nearly a year later, I received a phone call and the man on the other end of the phone asked if I knew who was responsible for giving him a room for the night about a year before. At first, I had no idea what he was talking about, as I had put more than a few up for the night. I finally recalled that evening when he described the incident further. He exclaimed, "I must tell you what has happened!" He told me of how he had suffered for quite some time with the paralysis until he attended a worship service in Bradenton on New Year's Eve. He explained that as they worshiped the LORD, he felt as if a blast from a lightning bolt hit him. There was a sharp pain in his left arm, the arm that had been left useless from the stroke. He looked over at his arm and it was raised high up in the air! He got very excited and looked at his leg. It was still shriveled and paralyzed. One week later, he was worshiping in the same church when a 'lightning bolt' hit him again, this time in his leg. He declared, "I looked at my leg and saw the flesh fill out. I jumped up and ran around the church. And I have been healed ever since!"

He went on to tell me what had happened since his healing. He became a Boy Scout leader over a large troop of boys and had led about fifty of them to Jesus in the recent months. This man accepted my invitation to come out to the retreat and share his testimony.

In another encounter, I received a phone call from Bradenton. A young man said he was being harassed by demons. As I spoke with him, his voice suddenly changed and became what I would describe as a low growl. I thought at first he was just pulling my leg, but I continued to listen. He was asking for help. I did not feel like I could minister to his needs on the phone, so I invited him to come out to the retreat, listen to our conference speaker and receive ministry. He countered, "I do not have any transportation." I would not let that stop him from getting help, so I offered to come into town and pick him up. I thought he was just making excuses not to come. To my surprise, he said he would appreciate the ride. So that evening, I drove to his house in Bradenton and picked him up. We talked and just got to know each other on the way out to the retreat. He asked me several times to pray for him. It just wasn't the right time yet, so I kept driving. When we arrived, the evening meeting was about to begin. I brought him to sit near the front and sat next to him. I positioned myself with the aisle on my left and him on my right.

We sang the praise and worship songs, they received the offering and the speaker began to preach. This young man again asked me to pray for him, but I told him to wait. I thought perhaps he would respond to the altar call and receive his deliverance. He started to fidget uncomfortably but I had him penned in. When the altar call was given, he did not respond.

We walked out to the lobby after the service and talked with some of the students for a while. When almost everyone had gone home, we walked to the carpeted area under the covered carport entrance. One or two students were still nearby. I turned to him and said, "I would like to pray for you now." When I laid my hands on him and began to pray, he fell to the ground writhing and twisting up, almost like a pretzel. His eyes rolled back in his head, and he began foaming at the mouth. I knelt beside him. As I reached my hand toward him, he used his hand to strike at me like a snake even though his head was turned the other way and he could not see me. This made the hair on the back of my neck stand on end, but I would not be deterred. I rebuked the spirit that bound him and it came out. I knew the spirit had left when he relaxed, opened his eyes and looked at me with peace on his face. As soon as his voice became normal, he sat up and I helped him to his feet.

I used this experience to instruct the students. I believe God knew that they were ready for this understanding, and He had made me wait until nearly everyone else had left. I took the young man back to his home and used that time to teach him. I kept in contact for a while and bought him a Bible so he could continue his growth in God.

Many other experiences also took place. However, I need to tell you of another sort of training that God was doing in my life.

Chapter 10

IMPARTATIONS FROM MAJOR MINISTRIES

With a different major ministry coming to the retreat each week, I had the blessing of being exposed to them all. Some of them I had heard of before and some of them I had not. There were many that I enjoyed very much and a few that I wasn't so sure about. However, I learned from each of them and every single one left a deposit in my life.

I learned that not all ministries are always as 'holy' as they appear on television or on the platform. I will withhold the name of the first ministry. The first thing that disappointed me about them was that they would not fulfill their 11:00 a.m. teaching time, stating it was too early in the morning for them. This ministry was scheduled to do a concert on Saturday evening. Our practice was to receive an offering at the concert that went entirely to the guest artist. However, we always counted the offering, deposited it in our account and then a check was cut for the entire amount. We always rounded up the amount to make it even.

This ministry, however, insisted that they count the offering themselves. They wanted to deposit it straight into their account. I was amazed at their mistrust, thinking we would not be honest and give them the full offering. To give them the benefit of the doubt, perhaps they had been other places where the host did not follow through with what they said they would do. I had elevated all ministries on such a high pedestal that I couldn't believe this would happen.

I was blessed beyond measure by my years at Christian Retreat having sat under some of the greatest nationally known ministries. Even beyond that, I often moderated the services and assisted these ministries as they prayed for people. I have written here about several of them at the risk of sounding as if I am name-dropping. My intent is to share with you those who deposited their lives and revelations into my life. One such minister was Benny Hinn.

Benny Hinn came to Christian Retreat at least once per year. There was always great anticipation when he was on the schedule. As we sang and worshiped our LORD with total abandonment, the unmistaken presence of Almighty God would fill the tabernacle. I remember one night when a woman with very thick glasses was healed suddenly and miraculously. Benny called her to the platform. She stood there and read from a small print Bible without her glasses.

Another time, a woman was slain in the Spirit early in the service and stayed there until late in the evening. We literally had to carry her home so her friend could put her to bed. She came into my office the next day and told me she had not moved all night. She had experienced heavenly visions and related them to me. She said the heavy weight of God's glory had actually compressed her bed mattress and left an imprint of her body after she got up.

One night, Floy Cox and I were moderating the service for Benny. He suddenly stopped what he was doing and shouted in a very authoritative voice, "TOM, FLOY, COME QUICKLY!" We responded immediately! The fear of the LORD was so intense. Benny boldly declared, "PUT OUT YOUR HANDS!" Floy and I put our hands out in front of us. Benny laid his hands on ours and said, "GO, GO TOUCH THE PEOPLE!" I went down the aisle, reaching as far as I could into each row and touched the people on their foreheads. Immediately all were knocked down into their seats. Honestly, my thoughts were, "Why are you falling down by the Spirit—just because Benny laid his hands on mine?" Nevertheless, I kept on going. I was learning that the anointing is transferable in a very real and tangible way.

Benny's ministry was not without controversy. When he started blowing on people and throwing his coat at them, many were upset. I had many questions about that myself, until later.

Sometimes after Benny ministered under such great anointing, it seemed as if he was attacked with many doubts. He would question himself about why he had done some of the things he had done. I am reminded of a scripture in 2 Corinthians.

> And lest I should be exalted above measure by the abundance
> of the revelations, a thorn in the flesh was given to me, a messenger
> of Satan to buffet me, lest I be exalted above measure.

Concerning this thing I pleaded with the LORD three times that it might depart from me.

And He said to me, "My grace is sufficient for YOU, for My strength is made perfect in weakness." Therefore most gladly I will rather boast in my infirmities, that the power of Christ may rest upon me. [Emphasis mine.]   (2 Corinthians 12:7–9)

Kay Gordon is a missionary to the Eskimos in the Canadian tundra. She has many testimonies of miracles in her travels to the cold North Country. It takes great faith for anyone to go to the unreached people. Kay went as a single woman with much opposition from her own church. Women were supposed to teach Sunday school and things like that, but not become missionaries. She told of having been treated with great respect by the Eskimo people. For example, when it came time to eat, they served the greatest delicacy to her, reindeer eyeballs. As she tried to stick a fork in and cut it with a knife, it flipped over and looked up at her! She had to swallow hard.

She preached and taught with great authority and gentleness. One night when I was moderating the service for her, she asked me to come up and help pray for the many people who had responded to the altar call. We started in the center of the room and moved down the line, she went to the left and I proceeded to the right. I prayed for several people.

Next in line was Kim, a young woman who lived at the retreat. As I was about to lay my hand on her head to pray, I heard the LORD say, "Blow on her!" I said to the LORD, "Oh no. Things like that are for Benny Hinn to do." Immediately I felt the anointing of the LORD begin to lift. I said, "Wait! Okay LORD, I will do it, but this better work!" Imagine telling the LORD that. I took a breath and began to blow very, very gently. The instant I saw her hair move slightly from my breath she gasped and fell to the floor. I was shocked! I recovered and moved on to the next person. I took a quick breath and blew a little harder. You see, he was a big guy and I thought it would take more wind. How naive can you get? He stood there like a rock. Why? The LORD did not tell me to blow on him. What God wants is obedience. He will not be put in a box so we can say, "This is how you do it to get results."

Charles and Frances Hunter were among other ministers who came to the retreat. Now they were a trip. Frances told us of the time she read about tithing shortly after she had received the LORD. She figured up how much back tithe she owed. It was a very large amount, but she gave it immediately. Since that day, God has blessed her beyond measure. They told of how they would pray for people in the airports, or on the street or wherever they met them. They led multitudes of people to the LORD and many, many more into the Baptism of the Holy Spirit. There were untold numbers of miracles in their ministry. I was struck by the simple way they spoke. God explains this in I Corinthians.

> *But God has chosen the foolish things of the world to put to shame the wise, and God has chosen the weak things of the world to put to shame the things which are mighty;*
> *And the base things of the world and the things which are despised God has chosen, and the things which are not, to bring to nothing the things that are,*
> *That no flesh should glory in His presence.*
>
> (I Corinthians 1:27–29)

There were so many more great ministries that I had the privilege of sitting under and getting to know. However, I began to be stirred in another way.

Chapter 11

"THIS IS A TEST"

I would preach periodically at other churches in the Bradenton area. One of them was the church that was forming at Sun City Center, one-half hour north of the retreat. If you recall, this was the same place that Gerald asked me to join the staff at Christian Retreat. After I had preached there several times, they began to ask if I would come and be their pastor. I thought about it from time to time but did not consider it very seriously.

Several times, I have mentioned about how God led me through the language of dreams. I dream almost every time I fall asleep, but some of them are very significant.

God gave me another important dream. In this dream, I was driving a bulldozer preparing a building site for a church at Sun City Center. When I awoke, I interpreted this to mean that God was calling me to pastor there. I started thinking and praying more about that possibility. One day the Sun City Center Church leaders asked Gerald if he would send me there to be their pastor. He said, "No, he is not ready yet." I was crushed. I thought I was ready, but why didn't he?

Did you ever notice when you were in school that the teachers talked every day until they handed out the tests? Once the teachers handed out the tests, they remained silent. How does that relate to the tests God gives us?

As time went on, I seemed to forget about the dream until one day when it returned to my mind. That was strange, because when God gave me a dream previously, it always intensified as time passed. I asked God, "What's up? Why did I think You wanted me to go and be their pastor?" I received no answer. So, I asked again and waited. And then I asked again and waited. I asked a third time… and again, I waited.

God finally answered, "This was a test. I wanted to see if you would be willing to go. You have passed the test."

Later, God spoke to me in another dream about 'The Tabernacle of Ohio.' I had taught on "The Tabernacle of David," but what was this? I prayed and searched Scripture regarding what this could possibly mean. I decided to check it out as much as possible.

And so, we took a trip to Ohio to visit family and friends. On the way home, we visited Oberlin, Ohio, to see the place where Charles Finney had his ministry. A building called Finney Chapel now belongs to Oberlin College. It was built by the Finney family as a memorial to Charles. Shirley and I went into the building to pray. We walked through the basement and saw a very old, ornate pulpit. I imagined that Charles Finney stood behind that pulpit many times preaching his famous sermons. There was a huge, beautiful pipe organ. We went up into the balcony and admired the structure of the building with its open beams and beautiful wood. Then I walked up and onto the stage. I looked out over the pews and prayed, asking God if He wanted me to move to Oberlin and start a church. I received no specific answer.

We went to town and asked where the most popular local restaurant was, desiring to get something to eat and talk to some locals. You can usually find someone willing to talk. We did. He seemed to be the self-appointed official historian, just the person I was looking for. Our new friend gave us much of the information I wanted. He told us that the building had been given to the college. It was currently being used for rock concerts, but no church services. That grieved me.

We left with no clear direction and headed for Toledo, Ohio, where we stopped at a Catholic seminary property that was no longer being used. It would have made a great place for a large church. It also had many classrooms that could have held an awesome Bible college and multi-purpose ministry. The chapel was beautiful and had a capacity for about 200 people. Again, a gorgeous pipe organ was there. We left without having received any specific direction. When God has placed a vision in your heart, it is wise to investigate all of the possibilities by going to that place and walking on the property.

After visiting family for a while, we started our trip back to Florida, checking out one more place on the way. God had spoken the name of Zanesville, Ohio, in a dream. We stopped in this city and just drove around praying. We drove up a small mountain on one side of town and looked out over the city. We saw a radio tower across town on another small mountain, so we drove over there as well. A very nice building was being constructed for a restaurant. It would have made a wonderful church. There was still no direction concerning the 'Tabernacle of Ohio.' I finally placed it aside. Perhaps one day I will understand God's intentions.

Chapter 12

ON THE ROAD AGAIN

Many people told me they thought I had a pastor's heart. However, I saw myself more as an evangelist. The idea of traveling in a motor home all around the United States of America and Canada greatly intrigued me. I told Gerald of my growing desire to do some traveling. He suggested that I go as an ambassador representing Christian Retreat and the I.O.M. We announced this plan at convocation in 1987. Several pastors expressed interest in me speaking at their churches. In the next few weeks, my itinerary filled up. We found a school bus that had been converted into a motor home and launched out.

I had heard several other ministers tell of their 'war stories' in the traveling ministry. We planned a trip that would take us up the East Coast all the way to New England. Then we would travel up to the Canadian Maritime Provinces, back down to New York and across Pennsylvania, into Ohio. From there we would go to the Canadian province of Ontario, followed by Michigan, Indiana, Kentucky, Tennessee and Georgia. On our final leg of travel, we would return to Florida. I was so excited.

We headed north, towing our little car behind the motor home, preaching, singing and worshiping God wherever we went. Shirley was going to home school our two youngest children, Todd and April.

God had given me a revelation concerning the "Tabernacle of David." I preached this same message almost every place we stopped. By the time we returned home, Todd said, "Dad, I think I could preach that message as well as you."

Georgia was our first stop. I preached on the second floor of a casino on St. Simons Island. Pastor Bill Ligon was starting a satellite church there named St. Simons Christian Renewal Church. We enjoyed good ministry and I got to know Bill and his associates better. We had met at Christian Retreat when he came as the speaker one week each year.

When we were ready to leave Brunswick, our motor home wouldn't start. Our journey had begun... and so had the problems. We prayed. A guy saw me looking at the engine, came over and offered to help. He drove me to an auto parts store. We purchased a new fuel filter and got it installed. It finally started, but didn't run very well. I didn't find out until later that I needed to bleed the air from the injectors. [This motor home had a Perkins diesel engine that was located in the rear of the bus.]

Our next stop was in North Carolina with Bill Cote, one of the students I had the privilege to speak to in the I.O.M. He had started a small church and it was growing. We ministered in Virginia in an old theater building that was converted to a church. Ron Hall was pastoring a church in Ladysmith, Virginia. He also had invited me to preach at his church. We ministered in New York, Massachusetts, New Hampshire and Maine. From there we crossed over the border into New Brunswick, Canada. Jim Divine and his wife, Diane, had set up an itinerary throughout New Brunswick that kept us busy for several weeks. I spoke at Full Gospel Businessmen meetings, jails, churches and home Bible study groups. Our children, Todd and April, enjoyed getting to know the Divines and played computer games with them.

We ministered about one month in New England and Canada before heading south, through Upstate New York. We took a day off and went horseback riding. I rode a spirited horse and Shirley was on a very gentle old nag. I came up behind her and slapped my reins on her horse to make it go a little faster. I thought that was fun, but she wasn't all that thrilled about it.

We stopped in Buffalo, New York, where Pastor Tommy Reid had a large church. He had been to Christian Retreat several times. Since I had gotten acquainted with him, it was nice to visit again.

We crossed into Conneaut, Ohio, and stopped to visit a woman I had led to the LORD at Christian Retreat. When we first met, she had been traveling through Florida and found that the motels at the interstate exit near the retreat were all full. One of those hotels told her about Miracle Manor motel located on the grounds at Christian Retreat. She came and checked in for the night. Someone invited her to go to the meeting that evening in the tabernacle. Following the service, she asked me if the Jesus they were talking about was the one in the Bible. She didn't have a clue about the Gospel.

In the process of explaining things to her, she accepted the LORD as her own Savior. I had sent her a Bible to help her on her journey with Jesus.

We arrived at Archbold, Ohio, and spent some time with our families. We had planned to take a day to go to the lake with my parents, brothers and sisters. They were going to ride with us in our motor home. No more than twenty miles down the road, the radiator fan went through the radiator and we lost the coolant. Change of plans. New radiators for a bus like that are expensive, but somehow God provided.

We traveled on up into Michigan and preached at a church near Detroit. The pastor there had been saved during the hippie revival. I was having the time of my life. This was what I was meant to do, or at least I thought so. Shirley wasn't so sure. She never wanted to be a schoolteacher. She started to suggest that God might want us to settle in one place and enroll the children in school. That was the beginning of God getting us ready for the next leg of our journey.

We drove north out of Detroit heading for Little Eden, a church camp operated by the Mennonite church. We had a flat tire on the motor home. We had to unhook the car we were towing in order to back up and get the tire repaired. When we finished, we hooked up the car again. I attached the safety chains but unfortunately forgot to latch the hitch down. You guessed it. We were going about fifty-five miles per hour on North I-75 when I felt a jerk. The car had come unhooked. I cried out, "JESUS!" as I looked in the rear view mirror to see our car doing 360 degree circles on the interstate behind me. Cars were swerving everywhere, but no other vehicle was hit. Our car finally hit the guardrail just before it came to a stop. There was some damage, but I was able to pull the fender off the tire, hook it back up to the motor home and proceed down the highway.

Why did I tell you that? I want you to know that even when we mess up, God is merciful. He watches over us and protects us. We took several days off at the church camp to relax and enjoy some old friends. Shirley and I had managed the camp a couple of years earlier, so this was a special time for us.

We continued our ministry on down through Ohio, Kentucky, Tennessee and into Georgia. We arrived back in Bradenton, Florida, at the end of

November. Suddenly it seemed that our places to go just dried up completely. "It is hard to find places to go to preach near Christmas," I pondered. However, when January came I still had no places lined up to speak. Several times, I went to the phone to call some pastor friends to ask if I could come. Somehow, I just couldn't do it. I believe it is God's responsibility to arrange our schedule. I had told Him back when He first spoke to me in the Fulton County Jail that I would go wherever He sent me. I didn't want to step out of His will by manipulating my schedule.

Mid-January arrived and I was getting concerned. I still had no place to preach. To take care of my family I needed to get going. I went over to visit Bud Hitt, my spiritual father, and asked him to pray with me. Within a couple of days, I received a phone call from Hampton, South Carolina, to come and preach for a weekend. I thought, "Now things are starting again and I can continue my ministry as a traveling evangelist." I couldn't wait to tell Bud.

When I told him about the invitation to go to Hampton, he prophesied that I would meet the most hospitable people I had ever met. He was right. On February 6, 1988, we arrived in South Carolina for the Sunday service on February 7th. That morning I met people who were very friendly. They seemed like my kind of down-home people. This one lady, Gloria Jones, came into the prayer room and introduced herself to me by saying," Hi. I'm the church idiot." I was certainly surprised but recovered and quickly bantered, "Well, according to your faith, be it unto you." We became very good friends.

The name of this church was Higher Ground Christian Fellowship. I expected to preach on Sunday morning and Sunday evening and then move on to the next place. They were looking for a new pastor, but I was an evan-gelist. I was happy traveling all around the country to minister. Do you remember how Shirley had said she felt that God wanted us to settle down in one place where we could enroll our children in school? Well, I preached that morning and in the afternoon, the deacons had a meeting with me. They asked if I would consider coming as their pastor. I replied, "I will do whatever God wants me to do." However, I did not think He would want me to be their pastor. They said the congregation would have a vote the next Sunday and they would get back to me.

I preached again that evening and went to sleep for the night. In the morning, I noticed God had been already at work changing my desires. Psalm 37:4–5 encourages, "Delight yourself also in the LORD, and He shall give you the desires of your heart. Commit your way to the LORD, trust also in Him, and He shall bring it to pass."

Some people interpret that scripture to mean that whatever we desire to have, God will give to us. I see it differently. When we delight ourselves in God, He takes His desires for us and puts them into our hearts. Therefore, our desires become the very thing He desires for us.

On Monday, February 8th, I made an appointment with a real estate agent who attended that church just to look around at what the cost of renting or buying a house would be in that area. We stayed overnight Monday and headed to Florida on Tuesday. All the way, we kept talking about what we had seen and what the possibilities were for ministry there. God had totally changed my heart in one day. Yet, even if they called me to come, I still wanted to know whether it was God. I asked Shirley, "Would it take an 80% vote, a 90% vote or how will we know if it is God?"

You may begin to see a pattern here. I had learned to trust God when He spoke to me in a dream, especially when it came to major new directions for my life. The congregation was to vote on February 14th. When I woke up that morning, Shirley told me that she had experienced a dream. She dreamed that they voted, and all but one had voted for us to come. I said with confidence, "That is good enough for me." But, I didn't stop to think how I would ever find out how many did or did not vote for us.

We went to Sunday morning services at Christian Retreat and that afternoon I got a phone call from one of the leaders at Higher Ground Christian Fellowship. He said, "We voted this morning and we would like to extend an official call for you to come to Hampton, South Carolina, to be our pastor." I thanked him, said I would be praying about it and would call him back soon. He said, "Well, if it makes any difference, everyone in the church voted for you to come but two!" I said, "Thank you," and hung up.

I immediately said right aloud, "God, how come Shirley's dream said everyone voted for us to go but one and this man said everyone in the church voted for us but two?" God is so good. He immediately said,

"It was a husband and wife, and I saw them as one." Well I knew that was biblical, so that settled it completely. About two years later, I did find out who it was, and of course, it was indeed a husband and wife.

We traveled again to Hampton, South Carolina, for the February 21st weekend and ministered again. I had a commitment to do a wedding in Florida on February 28th so our time in Hampton was limited. Before we returned to Florida, we looked around for a place to live. The first house we looked at had an efficiency apartment attached. We liked it very much. The realtor had several more houses to show us, but we always compared them to that first one. I thought we needed the apartment for a 'prophet's chamber' for visiting preachers to use when they came to minister for us. One of the deacons, a businessman who had a good relationship with the local banker, suggested he could arrange for us to make an offer on the house we liked. All we had was $50.00. We gave him the money and made the offer. They accepted it and the bank approved it. Who said that God couldn't do the impossible?

Once again, we were off on another leg of our journey with the LORD.

Chapter 13

MARCHING ORDERS

Our two oldest children, Tyler and Tony, had grown up and were living on their own. Shirley and I, along with our two younger children, Todd, age fifteen, and April, age twelve, packed our bags for the move. Todd was not happy about moving at all. South Carolina was so far away. He had friends in Florida and would not ever get to see them again.

I drove the rental truck and Todd rode with me. Shirley drove the car while April kept her company. I tried to cheer Todd up as we traveled but was not very successful. I sang some old songs and tried to joke with him, but he was in no mood for it. There was a girl in Florida he thought was nice, and he just knew that for as long as he lived he would never be happy again.

We moved into a mobile home for one month until the mortgage papers were ready at the bank. Immediately we got busy about our Father's business. The mobile home we lived in had been a parsonage for a church that had since disbanded. A couple who had been leaders in that church, but did not even attend Higher Ground, came to see us. They said God had told them to give us a sizable donation to close the checking account for that church. We applied that to the down payment for our house. God was confirming to us His willingness and ability to supply all of our needs according to His riches in glory by Christ Jesus.

We had not been in Hampton very long when I began to learn about the history of South Carolina. I discovered that South Carolina had seceded twice from the union. It is important to know the history to be able to minister in a community. There are territorial spirits that must be dealt with if you are going to be successful.

Again, I had a dream with a message from God. In the dream, there was a giant thick wall. It looked like the Great Wall of China. I was holding a large tree log as a battering ram. [In a dream, anything is possible.] I was holding it over my head by handles that looked like bicycle handle bars. There was a long thin shaft, like a needle, that extended from the butt of the log. That prod was as long as the wall was thick. I ran toward the wall and rammed the wall with the battering ram. The prod pierced one-third of the way into the wall. I backed up and ran at the wall again. The prod hit the exact same spot and this time pierced two-thirds of the way into the wall. I backed up the third time and ran at the wall, hitting the exact same spot. This time the prod pierced all the way through the wall and the butt end of the log hit the wall and knocked it down. Then the LORD said, "There are three major barriers that must be destroyed in this area. The first is the racial barrier. The second is the denominational barrier. The third is the social barrier." Then the dream ended. I had my marching orders for my ministry in Hampton.

I was invited, as the new preacher in town, to attend the Martin Luther King rally in February for the commemoration of the birthday of this leader of the civil rights movement. I was given opportunity to pray the opening prayer. When the meeting started, I noticed that I was apparently the only white face in the building. Then the LORD dropped something into my heart. The revelation of identification prayer was given to me. When I got up to pray, I said, "Before I pray today, as the son of a slave owner, [because I am of the white race] I want to ask you, as the sons and daughters of slaves, [because they were of the black race] to forgive me." Then I prayed the invocation.

I was hammering at the racial barrier. I heard a few comments later, like, "I don't want my pastor asking people to forgive me. I never owned any slaves." I just ignored them. I reached out to all of the people in the community regardless of their color, beliefs or social standing. I was blessed to lead many to the LORD in the prayer of salvation.

Hampton County is considered the "Watermelon Capital of the World." Each year there is a festival in the county. The Watermelon Festival is the longest continuous running festival in South Carolina. There are many events for a whole week and then on Friday evening there is a street dance. I was told many people go to this event to see others they haven't seen for a year, while others only go to get drunk. I said, "What a perfect field for evangelism."

I proposed that we set up a food stand as a front from where we could sell ice cold Coca Colas and hot apple fritters while giving out tracts and blessing the people. We rounded up a crew and got them excited about it. They had not done anything like that before. We had a lot of fun and started breaking down walls.

We also built a float for the huge parade on Saturday morning. We put a generator and a sound system on the float. Our praise team turned up the music and we sang praise songs along the parade route, while a team of us walked along side, shook hands with people and handed out tracts of little red Bibles. I heard reports for years afterward of how people were blessed that day. One young girl who was confined to a wheelchair received a little Bible. She had some very severe medical problems and went to be with Jesus several months after the parade. Her father told me that his daughter had prayed to receive Jesus after reading that little Bible. He said she still had it until the day she died. Sometimes we never hear of the end results of our witnessing efforts, but it is very encouraging when we do.

Francine Smiley, a precious lady in the church who operated a Christian bookstore, didn't think she could walk the two-mile route because her knee cartilage was worn out. However, once she got started, she just got stronger and thoroughly enjoyed the whole thing. We continued this ministry for several years.

Another area of outreach ministry I felt led to encourage our congregation's involvement in was the prison ministry. A state prison had just been built about eight miles from the church. I knew how much it had blessed me when I went to the prisons of America to take the Gospel. I wanted my new church members to be blessed also.

In Matthew 25, we read the account of when Jesus taught us to visit the sick and those in prison. He said that when we do that, it is as if we are doing it unto Him. I would tell the congregation, "Just go once and if you don't want to go again, that is okay." I got many of them hooked that way. Several of them have thanked me time and again. We need to look outside of ourselves and to the needs of others to be really fulfilled in our ministry. God had sent me to touch the community with the Gospel of the Kingdom and not just to minister to a group of people within the four walls of the church.

One inmate, whom I will identify only by his nickname Bear, was incarcerated in the Allendale State Prison in South Carolina. He was born of Jewish parents and prayed in Hebrew. One day as I ministered to him, I was blessed to lead him to his Messiah, Jesus. He came regularly to the Bible study we held in the prison. He inquired about being baptized. The prison was in the process of obtaining a portable baptismal for us to use for those who wanted to be baptized. We made the arrangements, and Bear was the first inmate to be baptized in that prison. When he was re-leased, he came and lived in our house for nearly a year. I will have more to say about that later.

I believe that radio broadcasting is an effective means of communicating the good news of the Gospel of the Kingdom. Higher Ground began to sponsor a fifteen-minute radio program Monday through Friday. Tony Gross, the owner of WBHC radio station in Hampton, started introducing me as Pastor Tom because not many people could get used to the name of Nafziger. I was, after all, a "Yankee" who had come from Ohio to the heart of the Bible Belt. I have said that if the South is the Bible Belt, then South Carolina is the buckle of that belt.

We would have people call the radio station and ask for prayer from time to time. I became known in the community as 'that preacher on the radio.' I met a woman at a yard sale one day. She recognized my voice. When she heard me talk, she asked me if I was 'that preacher on the radio.' People from many different denominations would listen regularly to the program. We were banging away at that denominational barrier. I will get back to the radio ministry later.

There are many prejudices still remaining, but wherever we go, we keep tearing them down one by one.

Chapter 14

FIRED!

Malachi chapter 3:2–3 reads, "But who may abide the day of His coming? And who shall stand when He appeareth? for He is like a **refiner's fire**, and like fullers' soap: And He shall sit as a **refiner and purifier** of silver: and He shall **purify** the sons of Levi, and **purge** them as gold and silver, that they may offer unto the LORD an offering in righteousness" (KJV). [Emphasis mine.]

The word **"fired"** has two very powerful meanings for me. I share this next chapter for the express purpose of helping people understand that sometimes things seem like they are very bad, but God is at work. Romans 8:28–29 states, "And we know that all things work together for good to them that love God, to them who are the called according to His purpose. For whom He did foreknow, He also did predestinate to be **conformed** to the image of His Son, that He might be the firstborn among many brethren" (KJV). [Emphasis mine.]

I am reminded of the plastic animals I saw being molded one day. To be conformed to the desired shape, the heat was turned up high. The mold was clamped together with great pressure. Next, very hot liquid plastic was pumped into the mold. When the mold was completely full, it held the plastic in the shape of that mold while the coolant was circulated through it. After the plastic was conformed to the mold, the pressure was released and the mold opened. Out came a perfect duplicate of the original. Do you get the picture?

Joseph said in Genesis chapter 50 that what man intended for evil, God turned for good. I now understand that God loved me too much to leave me the way I was; so He used fiery trials and spiritual pressure to take me through a process of transformation.

One Sunday morning I was preparing the message God had deposited on my heart. In Joshua 3:7, I read, "And the LORD said to Joshua, 'Today I will begin to exalt you in the eyes of all Israel, so they may know that I am with you as I was with Moses'" (NIV). I believed God was telling me that He would establish me in this community before the people as their leader. Frankly, I was excited. I expected that now we would all be on the same page and could accomplish what God intended. Shirley was sick that morning so she did not go with me to church. She almost never missed a service.

I went to church with Todd and April. We had an incredible time of worship. We reached a higher place in the Spirit than normal. The presence of God was so precious. There was an utterance in tongues, one of the gifts of the Spirit. The Bible teaches that if anyone has an utterance in tongues, and there is no interpreter, that person should refrain from speaking. Our worship leader gave the utterance and the Spirit gave the interpretation to me. This was the interpretation: "Oh God, we love you. And we know that You love us. We know that You are very near, but there seems to be a fog and we cannot see You clearly. So I ask You to turn up the fire and burn off the fog."

I was trembling because of the awesome glory of His presence. The fear of the LORD came upon me. I pleaded with the people that if any of them were holding any unforgiveness, they needed to let it go.

What happened next totally shocked me. Some of the people became very angry. They shouted out. I took the cordless microphone to anyone who wanted to speak. Someone shouted from the balcony, "Why are you tearing up our church? Why don't you let the people go home?" I said, "Okay. You are all dismissed. You may go home." No one moved.

One dear brother read from Psalm 55:21a, "The words of his mouth were smoother than butter, but war was in his heart." He seemed to be suggesting that this message was for me. Our precious sister, Francine, pleaded with the people to recognize that the Spirit was doing something very special and we should all pray together.

Many other things were said; then, we finally ended the service. When I got home, I quickly told Shirley what had happened. I said, "Shirley, we need to pray for all of the people right now and forgive them. We cannot let this destroy us or any of the others by letting unforgiveness rule us."

Later that week, I was outside the house cutting the grass when two of the deacons stopped in front of the house and asked me if I was going to the deacons' meeting. I replied, "I didn't know there was a meeting, but I will go in and wash up and be there."

When I walked into the office, a surprised look appeared on many faces. They were obviously not expecting to see me there. There was some discussion. Then they were going to vote whether I should continue as the pastor. The vote was two for me to stay and three for me to go. The meeting ended.

I was disappointed and puzzled. Why would God send me to be their pastor at this church only for me to be let go? I knew this was not the will of God, but rather the will of men.

The next day I decided to look at the constitution and bylaws of the church. It was clear that the deacons did not have the authority to dismiss the pastor. They are an advisory board only. The trustees were the only individuals given authority to vote on such a matter. I made copies of the constitution for each of the members and distributed them. The next Sunday night we would have a members meeting.

There was considerable discussion and support expressed by members of the congregation. The large majority wanted me to stay on as their pastor. Some even started to circulate a petition on my behalf that many of them signed. I explained to them that according to the constitution the deacons did not have the authority to fire me.

The trustees decided to call a meeting for the next Tuesday evening and invited me to come. You see, I was not officially a deacon or a trustee. On my way to the meeting, I observed one of the trustees, a founding member who no longer attended the church, meeting with his son-in-law who still attended there.

When I arrived at the meeting, I was asked to remain in the outer office while they met in the inner office. The trustee I had seen on my way to the meeting entered the inner office with his son-in-law. He resigned as a trustee and the son-in-law was voted in as his replacement. He then left.

I was then invited into the inner office and asked to resign as pastor of the church. My answer was, "I cannot resign. If I resign, I would feel like I was resigning from God and I wouldn't do that." One of the trustees said, "I cannot believe that you would make us fire you!"

I replied, "I am not **making** you fire me. You don't need to fire me. In fact, you can't fire me because you did not hire me." They retorted, "Well, we can stop paying you," to which I replied, "But you are not my source. God is my Source!" I was amazed at the words I spoke and the peace that I had in the midst of this storm. I knew that God had brought me there and that was all I needed to know.

I asked, "Where in the Bible do you find the scripture that says that a group of people or a committee can fire a pastor?" They answered, "Well, it isn't there but we are going to do it anyway." I simply said, "Well then, do what you are going to do." They did. They fired me!

I asked them, "Will I be barred from coming to church here?" They said, "No, of course not. We do not bar anyone. But you certainly would not want to, would you?" My answer was confident, "I will be here. This is where God sent me, and this is where I will be until He tells me what to do next."

These people loved the LORD. I loved the LORD. People who love the LORD can still be guided at times by their own will. I can look back now and see that God was refining [firing] me, and I sincerely thank Him for it.

I called my pastor, Gerald Derstine, to ask for prayer and direction. He encouraged me and prayed with me.

In the ensuing months, I continued to attend church there. The leaders would bring in a speaker each Sunday. When the service would end, several people would come to me and ask me to pray for them. Of course, I would. Then I also asked them to keep my family and me in prayer. And I waited.

I worked some construction jobs to earn money so my family could eat and pay our bills. Some of the people helped us with monetary gifts. In all of this, God continued to supply all of our needs. However, after five months I was getting a bit anxious. I called Gerald again. He told me that he was speaking in Brunswick, Georgia, the next weekend with Pastor Bill Ligon. Shirley and I decided to go. I knew Bill Ligon very well, so I called him to see if I could meet with him and Gerald for counsel. He also had met with the leaders from Higher Ground.

When we met, we prayed together. Then they asked me some questions. I told them that several of the people in the congregation were asking me to hang on because they were expecting me to come back as their pastor. I remember very clearly how Gerald prayed. He said, "LORD, help Tom recognize that Your way up is down." Huh???

After the prayer Bill said, "My words of counsel to you are that you should go back and say to the leadership there that you are no longer a candidate for pastor there." I did not want to do that! I knew that God had sent us to Hampton. How could I say that?

In the car, on our return trip to Hampton, Shirley asked me about the guidance Gerald and Bill had given me. When I told her, she asked, "Are you going to do that?" With tears running down my face, I blurted out, "Yes! I don't want to, but I respect the counsel of Gerald and Bill. I recognize them as men of God. I trust them. So I will do as they have suggested."

I immediately went to the leaders at the church and told them that I was no longer a candidate for pastor there.

I did not realize how much that was going to set me free. In a few days, I heard from God. He said to me, **"Your work in Hampton is not yet complete. I want you to start a new work here."** Do you remember the marching orders God had given me? There was still more work to do.

I was so relieved. I finally had heard from God and I knew what I was to do next. Because of my belief in doing all things in order, I went to the church leadership again and told them what God had said. I did not want them to hear it from someone else. They responded to me by saying, "We want you to get up and announce this to the congregation this Sunday evening."

When I stood before the congregation to make my announcement, I said, "God told me my work in Hampton is not yet complete. I will be holding service at the Fun Wheels skating rink next Sunday. Ask God what you should do. If He tells you to stay here, do that and support this work with all your heart. If He tells you to work with me, just obey God." Then I sat down.

After the service, the same people who had fired me five months earlier, came to me, handed me a check for $1,000.00 dollars, and said, "Here, this is to help you start your new work." I believe they recognized that it was not my intent to tear down their work. I just wanted to do God's will for my life.

Years later, I got to know Marvin, a man who lived in that community. He confided, "Tom, when you got fired and you didn't leave town, that day you gained my respect." God had truly established me as a leader in this community.

Chapter 15

FREED TO SERVE

The following week, I did not call any of the former members to ask them to join me in my new ministry work. Shirley and I sat down and wrote the names of the families we thought might come. When we looked at that list some time later, we found that all of them had indeed come and worked with us. Thirty-five people showed up that first Sunday, including a few people I had not met before. I still don't know how they knew about the new church. Francine told me, "When I left home this morning, I still didn't know where I was going to go for church. When I got to the corner and had to turn one way or the other, I did not hesitate. Here I am."

We set up chairs, located a podium and started worshiping the LORD. When I preached, I started by encouraging the folks to look forward and not look back. That is what we did. I was reminded of the dream God had given me about the three walls or barriers that needed to be destroyed. We set about to destroy them.

I would visit people at every opportunity regardless of their race, color or creed. I had a new freedom I had not known before. Willie Lawton invited me to a family reunion of an interracial couple. I had led Willie to the LORD and had baptized him while pastoring at Higher Ground. In South Carolina, interracial marriages are a major challenge for most people because of the long-term prejudices. People in the South seem to have a built-in respect for preachers, so I was asked to pray the blessing on the food. When I took my plate around the table to dish up my meal, I would ask them what some of the foods were. I recognized the pulled pork. However, when I got to the next dish and asked what it was, they said, "You don't want to know." They called it 'hash'. I took some, and it was good. Later they told me some of the things they put in it, everything that was left from the pig 'but the squeal.' Times like this formed a good rapport with the African American community.

In the summer, we had a float from which we played Gospel music. We used it for outreach ministry as we travelled to other nearby towns. My vision to reach a larger community was growing. I knew a song that summed up our mission. It had these phrases in it:

We are able to go up and take the country,
And possess the land from Jordan to the sea.
Though the giants may be there our way to hinder
Our God has given us the victory.

For our purposes, I changed the words to meet the community and surrounding area we lived in:

We are able to go up and take the country,
And possess the land from Kline to Yamassee.

These were two nearby towns, with Kline to the west of us and Yamassee to the east. It made the song much more personal to us. We would sing on the parade route and others would walk along and shake hands with the people while they handed out tracts and blessed them.

We participated in several South Carolina festivals including the Water Festival in Beaufort, the Rice Festival in Walterboro, the Schutzenfest in Erhardt and in the Cooter Festival in Allendale. We won several trophies for the first place float in these parades. I believe it was not because we had the best-made float, but because of the anointing that was with us. More importantly, we were spreading the joy of the LORD and the message of the Kingdom of God wherever we went.

My relationship with the owner of the radio station WBHC opened the door to expand the radio ministry. We leased the AM station for all Gospel programming. We held a live Share-A-Thon remote broadcast at the gazebo in downtown Hampton. People going by in their cars honked their horns and some of them stopped to donate for the operation of the Gospel programming. We encouraged the participation of folks from across denominational lines, another blow against that barrier. We also expanded the programming to a couple of hours each day on the FM station.

The following year, when the Watermelon Festival time came around again, we built a display on our float that included a radio tower and miniature water towers with the names of area towns on them. Then we took streamers from the top of the radio tower to the tops of the various water towers to show the reach of our Gospel programming. We called the DJ's who played the music on the radio "Air Ministers." One of these air ministers played music as we traveled the parade route.

We had a wide variety of air ministers during the years we sponsored the radio work. One of these was the former inmate, Bear, the person I mentioned earlier who came to live with us when he was released from prison. Another was Rachael from Booger Bottom, Georgia. [No kidding!] My associate pastor, Charlie Lightsey, doubled as an air minister and advertising salesman. He was a native of Hampton County and knew everyone. He did a terrific job and increased our sponsor base.

Charlie and I became a real close team. We did everything together. On July 4th, we decided to put on a fireworks display for the community at the downtown gazebo. Our church choir prepared a medley of patriotic songs to present to the people who came out. We borrowed a huge forty-foot by thirty-foot United States flag and hung it on the side of the Hampton Town Museum. You should have seen Charlie and me up on the roof of that museum building, hanging over the edge, fastening the flag so it wouldn't fall down during the show. We put a pulley up in the pecan tree next to the building so we could pull an old wooden cross up during the performance. Next, we asked a town policeman to position his car so he could shine the spotlight on the flag at our signal. When we were singing "Lift High the Cross," a Hosanna Music song, we had the police officer turn on his spot light and a shadow of the cross fell across the flag. You could almost hear the gasp out of the crowd that had gathered. We had communicated our message. "We Need God in America Again," as Carmen stated it in his song.

After the singing ministry portion of the event, we put on a fireworks display. This was the platform God had given us to draw people to the event. It was so well accepted that we decided we would do it again the following year at the Varnville gazebo.

This time we were directed to serve communion as part of the event. We started with a concert of contemporary Gospel music. The medley of songs included the Hosanna music song with lyrics concerning the wine and the bread. As we sang, ushers passed out the elements and we served communion to approximately 500 people. They represented many of the church denominations. It was really a healing time for our community. We also had a special ceremony honoring our returning Gulf War troops. Again, we had the huge flag raised with a crane as a backdrop during the concert. Our friend Bear was there to help light the fireworks. We had delivered another blow against the barrier of denominational separation.

Chapter 16

NEW HORIZONS

We continued to rent the skating rink for almost a year when the owner informed us that he wanted us to find somewhere else to continue meeting. Many times circumstances that arise seem to be bad. However, God is at work 'firing' us and developing us. His desire is not only to refine us but also to advance us into His ultimate purposes. Joseph (Jacob's son) had been sold into slavery, yet rose to great heights of power that allowed him to bless nations. When speaking to his brothers, Joseph said, "What you meant for evil, God meant for good." (See Gen 50:20.)

We started looking for a place for our worship services. We remembered the couple who had given us a gift from leftover funds from their church when it closed its doors. The building in which that church had met was still vacant. We rented that facility and continued to preach and teach the Kingdom of God. God's Kingdom places sold-out Christians in positions of authority so His ways are implemented in the society of this world. One way to prepare young people for this is to train them up in the way they should go and when they are old, they will not depart from it.

The people at Higher Ground Christian Fellowship, where I had pastored before starting the new work, decided to close down the Christian school at their facility. A dear sister, Jean Wagers, decided to pick up the leadership for the school. She needed a facility for that purpose. There was space for the school in the facility where we had started holding our services. We added a couple of walls, and she administrated the school there.

Our church, Community Faith Fellowship, the name God had given us, helped raise funds for the school and encouraged them in every way. Since I had some experience with benefit auctions, I volunteered to hold one. Many local businesses and individuals in the community contributed items. It was quite successful. Perhaps as many as twenty or twenty-five students benefited from the school under Jean's care.

As a church, we continued to grow over the next couple of years. Several members expressed their desire to look for a place we could purchase so we would not need to move again. About eight miles out in the country there was a church that was going to sell their fellowship hall and Sunday school building. They were planning to build a new facility and needed the old ones moved off their property. I went to the sealed bid auction with one of my deacons, Gerald Anderson. We bought the building for about $2,200.00. When I first got out of high school, I worked for a construction company that at times had moved buildings, so this concept seemed normal to me. Now we had a building and needed to move it in a short period of time, but had no property on which to put it. Sounds backward, doesn't it?

I began looking for a piece of property. In the back of my mind, I ultimately wanted to buy the skating rink where we had first started, but that was out of reach financially. However, there were approximately one-and-a-half acres of land adjacent to the rink. I went to the courthouse and found out that it was owned by a family that had inherited it from their ancestor's estate. I inquired of them if we could buy it for our church property. It took some time, but we were successful.

We purchased the property and prepared to move the former fellowship hall and Sunday school building onto it. We had to separate the building into two sections to move it. When we placed them on the new foundation, we built a new section between them for restrooms and an office. Our new facility would hold about 125 people. Although we were not finished with the building, we scheduled our Christmas celebration and invited a music group to sing at a dinner party. I believed construction would be completed by the time that date arrived. I will never forget that on the day of the party, the carpet layers were finishing as we carried in the tables and set up chairs for the meeting.

Chapter 17

FUN WHEELS AND HOLY ROLLERS

We were off on more adventures. We continued to build the Kingdom of God, and God continued to bless. The church grew and carried on with the parade and radio ministries. By the time we moved into the new facility, the Christian school had been discontinued. God helped us to pay off the property in about a year-and-a-half. We had grown to the point where we needed to organize our youth group more. I believed we needed to buy the skating rink, providing the perfect facility for a youth group as well as providing a great outreach to the area's youth. The property also had an Olympic-sized swimming pool and a children's wading pool. We intended to use this new facility to host events to reach out to the community. In the hands of God-fearing, Spirit-led people who were not ashamed to make waves, this facility could become a mighty weapon.

I had been given a mandate from God to break down barriers. One of the biggest barriers was the racial one. The only other swimming pool in the area restricted black people from entering. This was very hard for me to believe, but it provided another opportunity to destroy this stronghold.

As we met with our elders and deacons, it was decided we should go ahead. Yet they were reluctant to mortgage our property that had just been paid off. I felt sure that the bank would not loan us the money without the mortgage, but was willing to negotiate with the banker.

The owner lowered the price a couple of times and then made me an offer of $1.00 plus take over the mortgage. He had accepted the position as pastor of another church and just wanted to be free from the responsibility of the skating rink. This was a good deal. However, would the banker go along with it?

When I approached the banker, he said he would look into it. Just to show you how God can work, when the banker checked it out, he discovered that there had been an error the last time the owner had refinanced the property. The bank had failed to file a mortgage at the courthouse. They held a note and the owner was good for it, but the proper paper work was not filed. The banker was eager to allow us to assume the debt so he could file the mortgage. Isn't that amazing? When we actually signed the papers for the purchase, the previous owner would not even accept the $1.00 purchase price. Oh, by the way, the seller allowed us to operate the skating rink business for two weeks and to receive all of the proceeds before we even signed the papers. That provided us with operating cash for Fun Wheels Christian Recreation Center.

We brought a youth pastor on staff who also managed the skating rink for us. The skate business provided his salary and paid all of the mortgage payments. Therefore, it did not put any financial drain on the other operations of the church. Ain't God good?

We decided to name the youth group "The Holy Rollers." It helped us promote the skating rink. In addition, it took away the opportunity for others to call us 'Holy Rollers' as a negative euphemism. At the next parade, we borrowed a large skate car from the Stardust skating rink in Augusta, Georgia. Some of the youth who attended the rink skated behind it for the whole two-mile parade route. Awesome!

Another year we put a small swimming pool on the float with young children playing in the pool to promote the swimming activities at Fun Wheels Christian Recreation Center. It was hard for me to believe, but this swimming pool had been restricted to white swimmers only up until the time we purchased it. I had been taught all of my life not to be prejudiced concerning race. I also had the mandate from God to destroy the racial barriers that were so prevalent, especially in the South. We took off all racial restrictions and made it available to all people of all races. Pound! Pound! Pound! We kept hammering away against the barriers that needed to be destroyed just as God had shown me in the dream.

I contacted James Black of Camp Wildwood. He had established a two-week summer camp for the purpose of teaching young children to swim and partnered with us to use our pool. Many African-American children had been denied the opportunity to learn to swim simply because they were black. There had been several drowning-related deaths in the community that inspired James to do something about it. Camp Wildwood was not restricted by race either. We worked together for many years promoting interracial activities. After several years of leasing the pool for the two-week period in the summer, he had trained many young people as lifeguards. He now leases the pool for the entire summer and conducts swimming activities for several different groups.

Chapter 18

COMMUNITY CHRISTIAN ACADEMY

Due to the mandate God had impregnated in me through the dream, I was constantly looking for opportunities to break down walls.

Even though the Christian school had been discontinued for some time, the vision that had long been in the hearts of the people of Hampton was still alive. This school had been a desire long before I was sent to the community. I agreed with the idea. However, I also knew that I was not qualified or called to oversee that type of work as an educator or a principal. I also was aware of many churches that had started Christian schools, causing such strain that the churches folded. I told God that if He wanted me to start a school in the Hampton community, He would need to send someone with the ability and the desire to do so. Enter God's timing and His interesting ways.

Our youth pastor, Rodney, turned in his resignation in order to return to Florida where he had lived before coming to Hampton. That meant we needed to find another youth pastor. Bruce and Doris Fox were members of our church. They had brought their niece, Linda, from the Philippines several years earlier. After she finished high school in Hampton, she had attended Southeastern Bible School in Lakeland, Florida. There she met and married Marvin Smalley. They both had teaching degrees. I called and asked them if they were interested in coming to Hampton, South Carolina. After we talked several times, they decided to accept the position to be our new youth pastors.

They moved to South Carolina and took on the job as manager of the Fun Wheels Skating Rink along with their ministry to the youth. We also began discussions about starting a Christian school. By January, we made the decision to establish Community Christian Academy as an arm of Community Faith Fellowship, Inc. This launched the foundation work to open for the following school year.

The school started in 1999 with about twenty students in kindergarten through ninth grade. Each year we added a grade so that the student who was in the ninth grade continued until his or her graduation. We had students from many different church denominations, different races and from a variety of social backgrounds—another fulfillment of hammering at the barriers God had given us to destroy. Eventually the school grew to approximately sixty-five students. We had several students who received Jesus as their Savior while at the school. We kept on building the Kingdom of God in everything we did. This school continues today even though we turned it over to another ministry to carry the torch.

I have a pioneering spirit. I enjoy launching out into things I haven't done before and then releasing them into the anointed hands of others.

Chapter 19

LET'S EAT!

God is the God of ideas! Just allowing Him to direct our lives will produce some of the most exciting experiences and challenges ever.

God gave me an idea to help destroy the social barrier in the community. Everyone likes to eat. So we provided a free Thanksgiving dinner for all who would come. Did I mean that 'Whosoever will' could come? Yes! My hope was that people who would otherwise never sit down and eat a meal together might do so at this event.

When I first tried to explain my vision to Tony Gross at the radio station, he had a hard time understanding what I wanted to do. I wanted him to promote this event on the radio. He thought it was just for people who might not be able to have a turkey and ham dinner. I had to explain that we wanted the 'haves' and the 'have-nots' to sit down and share a meal together. When he finally understood, he willingly announced it on the radio. Some people from the community wanted to get involved. They donated turkey, ham or other food. We also invited people from the community to help serve the food, and many did. Two couples came as far as fifty miles away to help serve.

The first year we served over 400 meals. Each year it grew in numbers. During the last two years, more than 1000 meals were served in one day. Many people were blessed by meeting people they would not otherwise have met. We had scored another blow to the barrier wall.

Chapter 20

EXPANDING OUR BORDERS

The radio ministry had continued to grow. We were on the air from 6:00 a.m. until 12:00 noon on the AM station and for several hours in the evening on both the FM and AM stations.

One day, when I was on the air as one of the air ministers, the South Carolina news broadcast announced every hour, on the half hour, that hurricane Hugo was approaching. They had just said it was going to make landfall right at Hilton Head, which would have put it on a path straight toward us. I was inspired to say "No!" When the news was finished and I went back on the air live, I said, "I rebuke that storm and command it in the name of Jesus to turn to the north."

Thirty minutes later, the weather broadcast announcement said, "We don't understand why, but the storm has changed direction a couple of degrees and will not make landfall in Hilton Head, but rather at Charleston." That meant that it would not affect our area but, indeed, would go north of us.

I am sure that there were many people praying. However, God used my declaration on the airwaves for a purpose that I did not know about until a couple of years later. Gary, a good friend of mine, was the pastor at the Christian Church in Hampton. He was having difficulty understanding about the Baptism in the Holy Spirit. He was searching, however, for more truth in his own life. About two years after that storm, he told me that when he heard me rebuke the storm on the radio that day, he said to himself, "Yah right! Who does Tom think he is to talk like that?" However, when the storm turned, he had to admit to himself that there just might be more to what I had done than he understood. God has many ways of speaking to those who are honestly searching for more of Him.

Does that also speak to you right now? Be bold and ask Him to give you a greater knowledge of Him. The scripture says in James 1:5–6,

"If any of you lacks wisdom, let him ask of God, who gives to all liberally and without reproach, and it will be given to him. But let him ask in faith, with no doubting, for he who doubts is like a wave of the sea driven and tossed by the wind."

Then again in James 4:2b–3, it says, "You do not have because you do not ask. You ask and do not receive, because you ask amiss, that you may spend it on your pleasures."

Don't let the term "the Baptism in the Holy Spirit" scare you. From my own experience, I know that it simply means a total surrender to God's will and plan for your life. As I said earlier in this book, when God asked me the second question that day back in the Fulton County Jail, **"Do you see what I can do if you will just go?"** My answer was, "Okay Lord, I'll go." That day I totally surrendered to God's will and plan for my life.

I pray you will make that same decision and commitment right now. You see, I had held back because I did not want to be a missionary and go to Africa. My concept of God was that if I totally surrendered, He would make me go to the mission field. What I discovered is that He did not force me to become a missionary, but He changed my 'want to.' As I began to mature in my Christian life, I developed a <u>desire</u> to go to the mission field.

The Scripture tells us in Psalm 37:4–5, "Delight yourself also in the Lord, and He shall **give you the desires of your heart**. Commit your way to the Lord, trust also in Him, and He shall bring it to pass." [Emphasis mine.] That does not mean that He will give you anything you desire, but He will change your heart's desires.

The effort to carry out God's mandate of breaking down satanic divisions was constantly stirring in me. To continue to destroy the denominational barrier that God had shown me in the dream, I met with a local pastor. Together we contacted several of the other local pastors and asked them to meet us for coffee on Monday morning. There had been a Ministerial Fellowship years earlier, but it had disbanded. There were about five or six pastors who started to meet each Monday morning. We prayed together. We laughed together. We shared personal needs at times and basically just got to know each other outside the walls of 'church.'

If we as pastors cannot lay aside our denominational differences for the sake of uniting on the things we all agree on, how can we expect the people in the community to do it? Every church group or denomination has certain revelations that are a great benefit to the Kingdom of God. The Body of Christ is hindered because many people will not fellowship together and learn these truths. We started conducting "Unity Meetings" on the fifth Sunday each quarter at the pastors' various churches.

That Monday morning coffee continues today. There are no self-imposed pastoral restrictions required to attend. Several men who are just hungry for fellowship attend regularly. What I find is that each member has a revelation, and as he or she shares it with the rest, it gives others opportunity to add to that revelation. Everyone benefits.

There are other things that we as a church were involved in, but I started to get the 'itch' again. I have learned to recognize when God is getting ready to change our course. He creates uneasiness in us to prepare us for what is still ahead on our journeys.

Chapter 21

THE UTTERMOST PARTS OF THE EARTH

All of my life I have had an interest in third world missions. It's probably because my Aunt Vesta and Uncle S. Paul Miller were missionaries in India for at least forty-four years. I grew up hearing stories of their mission work.

One story was about a man-eating tiger that had terrorized the village where they were living. The village officials asked Paul to shoot the tiger. I will never forget it. I was quite young when they brought that tiger skin back from the mission field. It had the head of the tiger still attached with its mouth wide open as if it was roaring. I would lie on the floor with my nose right up to the mouth of that tiger and think about what it would be like to be a missionary. One time Paul and Vesta cooked us an authentic Indian dish called rice and curry. I didn't like it very much and got sick after eating it. Although since then, I have come to enjoy Indian cuisine very much.

About seventy-five years ago, Paul and Vesta's work included helping to organize the Union Biblical Seminary. The seminary was a cooperative effort between twenty-one different mission organizations whose goal was to provide an excellent school of biblical study for the native people in India.

After my experience in the jail in 1979, whenever I met someone from India I would ask them, "Do you know my aunt and uncle?" The question seems silly with more than one billion people living in India. What was the chance of one of them ever meeting my aunt and uncle?

One October, I was attending a conference in Brunswick, Georgia. One morning, two pastors from India were eating breakfast. I asked if I could join them. One of the men introduced himself as Pastor Daniel from the state of Kerala, India. I asked them if they ever heard of S. Paul and Vesta Miller. To my shock and surprise Pastor Daniel said, "He was one of my instructors when I attended the Union Biblical Seminary." Pastor Daniel then invited me to come to India to minister with him.

A few weeks later, I met another man from India, Pastor Moses Choudary, from Hyderabad. He ran a Bible school and orphanage there. He also knew my aunt and uncle and invited me to come to India to minister with him.

If that wasn't enough, while attending the Gospel Crusade Convocation in January, I met Sharath Bhushan. He is the national coordinator of Gospel Crusade ministers in India. He had taken some courses from the Union Biblical Seminary and... you guessed it. He knew my aunt and uncle. Sharath also invited me to come to India to minister with him. The next morning it was announced that Gospel Crusade was looking for someone to go to India to minister and work with Sharath's ministry there. It took a while, but I got the message and immediately volunteered.

Mac Owen and his wife Lollie (who recently went to heaven) were seasoned missionaries, having been in more than forty countries around the world. They were ordained Gospel Crusade ministers, just as I was. Mac and Lollie were planning to go to India, so I decided it would be good for me to travel with them on my initiation trip into mission work.

When I arrived in Madras and realized where I was, and what I was supposed to do, I wanted to get back on the plane and come home. What did I have to offer these people? The doubts were racing through my mind. I thank God that Mac and Lollie were there with me. There is great value in traveling with mentors.

I soon was able to overcome the doubts and began to enjoy the adventure of missions. After all, God had shown me what He could do if I would just go. We spent the night at the YMCA. The next day, Sharath met us and we boarded a train for the long journey to Vijayawada, in the Province of Andhra Pradesh. We rode on a very old railcar with wooden seats and many, let me emphasize, MANY other people. It was as if we had stepped way back in time.

On the first leg of our mission trip, we met three young college girls, Shri Devi, Meenokshe and Michelle. I asked them what their names meant. Shri Devi is the name of a female god in Hinduism. Meenokshe means 'fish eyes' and Michelle is a Christian name that was given her from some contact with missionaries. Michelle said she was a Christian. When I asked her what that meant to her, she had no answer. That led me to press the issue. Before very long, all three of them prayed to receive Jesus, the one and true God. Hallelujah! I had introduced my first souls to Jesus on my first mission trip. I was hooked. The doubts were gone. I was in my element and I knew it.

When we arrived at our first mission post in Vijayawada, we were given a very nice room to sleep in at the home of Pastor Moses Choudary. I was introduced to eating Indian-style with my fingers. They offered us silverware, but I wanted the full experience, so I put my fingers to the task. There was quite a trick to it. They showed me how to do it and I got the hang of it soon enough. I didn't starve. In fact, I came to like Indian food and its exotic spices very much.

We ministered at several different settings. Two of them were roof top meetings. Now understand the roofs are flat so it worked out well. We had a loudspeaker system and we sang while some played drums. Then we shared the Word. I was very impressed with the stability, strength and commitment of these ministries in India to which God was connecting me.

In the morning, I heard a street vendor calling out his presence. He brought fresh milk to our door. The Indian people are very gracious and I fell in love with them.

As I looked out over the area, I could see the great contrast of the rich and the very poor. The home we were in was quite modern. However, next door there were thatch roofed huts and women washing clothes by slapping them against a rock. Talk about culture shock! We saw rag pickers going through the garbage finding things they could use or sell to get something to eat. "Dear God, how can I reach these people with Your love?" My heart was broken. God was purifying my heart again with His purging fire.

We took the train on to Narsapur. From the train station, we got into a rickshaw to make our way to a school for the blind. The rickshaw was pulled by a man on a bicycle. I felt sorry for him. I mean, there I was, this overweight American, being pulled by a frail-looking Indian. I had never seen anything like that in my life. He may have looked frail, yet he was anything but. At the school, many children were totally blind. They would hold hands to walk from place to place. They were having a crusade tent meeting there. How could there be so many blind people?

We traveled on, this time in a bus. We drove for many hours until we came to a river. There was no bridge over the river, so we got into a small boat that did not look too safe. In fact, it reminded me of what I imagined a dugout canoe must be like. We made it safely across the river where we were picked up by Sharath's driver in a car. It had been another bone-jarring trip, but we finally arrived at Sharath's mother's house.

Her home also served as a children's home. One of the children climbed up a palm tree with a machete and cut down a coconut. Then he held it between his bare feet and chopped it open so we could drink some fresh coconut milk. Imagine, holding the coconut between his bare feet and chopping it with a machete. The safety folks here in America would faint in a panic. The milk tasted okay, but I didn't want too much of it. [I heard that it can act as a strong laxative.]

I was given a fairly small room that I could enter from the front porch. It was pretty hot, but had a ceiling fan. The bed had a one-inch thick mat on it for a mattress. I was in bed only a short time when the fan stopped. They do not have twenty-four hour electricity, so I enjoyed it when it was on. I had gotten ice cream to eat earlier in the day. It had been served in a unique plastic container that looked like a baseball. I had saved the container to take home as a souvenir. In the middle of the night, I heard this "crunch, crunch, crunch," but I didn't get up to look. In the morning, I found that a mouse or rat had chewed it in pieces. It really didn't bother me much. Neither was I bothered when I heard the monkeys running across the roof.

We sat on the front porch and watched the ox carts as they passed by. Across the road and little canal, I saw a shepherd coming with his small herd of goats. He stopped his herd to graze for a while right in front of our house. He selected one of the goats and disappeared over the hill. Soon he came back carrying the butchered goat, which he took to the market to sell or trade for other food.

We traveled from Sharath's mother's house to the Peniel Bible School in Razole where Sharath's church was located. There we held a tent crusade and ministers' conference. They fed all who came with big pots of food cooked over outdoor open fires. I was amazed at what these people were able to do with so little. What may seem like a small offering here in America goes a long, long way in India. Sharath is a very giving and loving man, always looking for ways to bless the ministers and churches he oversees.

When we finished our mission work there, we traveled north to Visakhapatnam, another city where they had set up some meetings. Again, we ministered the Word of God on several occasions, though we encountered some opposition. Still, we had a very successful time of ministry.

I was determined to visit the Union Biblical Seminary where my aunt and uncle had worked for so many years. It was all the way across India in the city of Pune. We boarded a train and rode for a day and a half to get there. When we arrived, they found out I was the nephew of S. Paul and Vesta Miller and really rolled out the red carpet for me. We joined the staff, faculty and students at a coffee break and visited with them for a while. We also toured the campus before we left. We were there only a half day, but it was very fulfilling for me.

Then we boarded another train and traveled one day south to the Province of Kerala to work with Pastor Daniel. Voice of Gospel is the name of the ministry based in Trichur, Kerala, which Pastor Daniel and Sister Lilly oversee. We visited the nearby site where legend says the Apostle Thomas landed in India after the crucifixion of Jesus. A sign is posted there with quite an interesting story on it.

The sign states that when Thomas arrived, he observed a Hindu priest standing in the water, picking up water in his hands and throwing it up in the air. Thomas asked him, "What are you doing?" His answer was, "I am giving an offering to one of my gods."

Thomas retorted, "I guess your god does not accept your offering because the water falls back into the sea. If I offer up an offering to my God, the one and only true God, He will receive it." With that, Thomas stepped into the sea, scooped up a double handful of water and threw it up into the air. The legend says that the water hung in the air for a short time and then went straight up into the heavens. The Hindu priest immediately was converted.

That was when Christianity was first introduced to India in the first century. Today Kerala has the highest percentage of Christian people in India.

Voice of Gospel has a Bible school, several churches and a ministry for children that is quite unique from most Indian orphanages. They are in fact, not orphanages, but Mercy Homes. In India, families are allowed to take in up to ten children without being licensed by the state. So according to the vision God gave to Pastor Daniel, his ministry sponsors Mercy Homes where families adopt ten children who have been abandoned or orphaned and raise them within the family unit. This way, the children know they are loved as part of a family instead of being labeled as orphans. More recently, they have been expanding this concept all over India and in other nations.

We spent several days ministering with Pastor Daniel and then traveled by train back to Madras for our flight home.

The time to return to the United States had come. We had traveled substantial distances and traversed many types of terrains on this journey. However, God had taken me further and higher than I could have ever dreamed or imagined. I was not the same.

I am looking forward to the next trip to India with much anticipation.

Chapter 22

GUARDS WITH MACHINE GUNS

Another place God took me was Nicaragua in Central America. At the invitation of Bob Armstrong of Love Link Ministries, we conducted several pastors' seminars where we taught the Kingdom of God throughout the country. We also preached on the weekends in various churches. Our national host was Pastor Daniel Ortega Reyes, a powerful man of God who is known throughout Nicaragua. Through his ministry, he is seeing the country turn to Christ.

Bob has been going to Nicaragua for many years, starting back when the "Freedom Fighters" war was raging. He had built relationships that continue to open doors for ministry today. The Latin culture is totally different from the Indian culture, so I had to learn all over again. And again, I experienced the refining fire of God. It seems like the devil never learns. When he tries to discourage me with thoughts that I don't have anything of value to minister to the people, I just remind him of what God said to me, **"Do you see what I can do if you will just go?"** If we try to take upon ourselves the responsibility that belongs to God, it will become stressful. However, if we just rely totally on Him and do what He tells us to do everything will be fine. Harald Bredesen, a man God sent all over the world, once told me, "Make it hard on God and easy on you."

On my second ministry trip there, our minister's group was invited to the compound of Tomas Borge, a former Sandinista leader. When we arrived, some of our team were taking pictures of the compound. However, we were met by men with machine guns who 'explained' to us that taking pictures was not allowed. It is hard for us to understand what it must be like to live in fear of being assassinated.

After security clearance, we were ushered into his home. He shared the initial vision to reform the nation and went on to explain how pride had entered in causing everything to get out of hand. We were able to minister to him and pray with him. He was quite moved as seen by the tears that ran down his face.

It is a good thing I enjoy tasting new kinds of food because each country has its own special cuisine and spices. I ordered a black sea bass dinner with native spices, and it certainly woke up my taste buds. Just thinking about it makes me salivate and want to take a drink of water to cool my tongue.

There is an added blessing when ministering in other nations like this. I have met many other ministers and built relationships with them from right here in the United States. The people in the Body of Christ are wonderful people. I meet people from all denominations and various streams of worship, but we all have one thing in common—a desire to see the Kingdom of God fill the earth as the waters cover the sea, just like Bible prophecy.

It amazes me to see how God is sending me to the uttermost parts of the earth with the message of the Gospel of the Kingdom. The verse of Scripture He has dropped in my heart is Luke 4:43, which says, "I must preach the kingdom of God to the other cities also, because for this purpose I have been sent." Now I understand why I am being sent to the uttermost parts of the earth.

Chapter 23

CREATING HOLY SITES

In 2000, while still pastoring Community Faith Fellowship, I took a mission trip to Israel with a tour group led by Dr. Gerald Derstine. He has made more than fifty trips to the Holy Land, taking tours and building relationships with many people there. The purpose of our trip, as he so clearly put it was, "To visit the ancient Holy Sites and to make new Holy Sites." He sees this accomplished by visiting the homes of people who have become believers, singing and worshiping with them and sharing the good news of the Kingdom of God. In this way, many family members have become believers and established their homes as Holy Sites.

I had wanted to visit Israel for many years to walk where Jesus walked and see the things He saw. There is a special attraction for any believer in Jesus. When you arrive, you feel like you have truly come to your homeland. Words cannot explain this adequately.

We traveled from the airport to many different cities and villages, meeting with families and sharing the good news. We witnessed many people come into the Kingdom of God. One highlight was when we went to Tiberius and took a boat trip on the Sea of Galilee. Gerald asked me to share a message while we were out on the sea. This is the same sea where Jesus walked on the water.

We took a bus way up to the Golan Heights to visit the home of an Arab brother who was with us. When we went into his home, we found one of his relatives lying on a floor mat. He had not been off his 'bed' for many days and could not keep any food down. His skin was all yellow and he was dying. We gathered around him, laid hands on him and prayed in the name of Jesus for his healing.

The Arab believers are very bold. They said, "OK, now it is time for him to get up," and they began to lift him up. I watched and took pictures as this man's skin returned to normal color and the biggest smile came on his face. He began to lift his hands in thanks to God and the men let go of him. I had just witnessed a miracle before my very eyes. This man was healed! He began to move about the house. We soon left on the bus but received a phone call later that day reporting that he had taken food and was able to keep it down. He was a farmer, so the next day he went out to work in the field, totally healed by the power of God.

The highlight of all the ancient Holy Sites we saw occurred when we visited the Garden Tomb. I stepped into the tomb to pray for a moment. It was very moving as was the experience of receiving communion just outside the tomb. Before we left Israel, we visited Bethlehem, the site of Jesus' birth. I would recommend that everyone go to Israel sometime.

Chapter 24

THE DEAF HEAR—THE DUMB SPEAK

God is so good! One day I was talking with my father about the places I was going and the things God was doing in my life. He asked me a very reasonable question. He said, "How do you think you can travel all over the world? You are not wealthy and you cannot afford to do that!" I thought, "That's true," but what I said was, "I have been taught that where God guides, He provides. And if it is God's will, then it is God's bill." He just shook his head.

I had Ebenezer Sefah from Ghana, Africa, come to speak at our church. I also had arranged for him to speak at another church in Hampton. It was my responsibility to introduce him to the congregation for the evening service. In the course of the introduction, I mentioned I would soon be traveling with Brother Gerald to Romania to visit the churches there.

A woman came up to me after the meeting and said, "When you mentioned that you will be traveling with Brother Gerald to Romania, I just whispered a prayer to God, 'God, I would like to travel with Brother Gerald to Romania,' and God immediately responded to me, 'You can send Tom!'" Then she told me she was going to pay for my plane ticket. She went on to say that God also had told her how much the fare was.

I thought this was a good way for me to know if God had really spoken to her so I asked, "How much did He say?" She informed me of the amount God had instructed her to pay. It was a few dollars more than the amount I had just put on my credit card to buy the airfare.

When she brought the check to my house she said, "I did not tell you everything God said to me that night. He also said I was to pay your fare for your next two trips after Romania, wherever you go."

When I told all of this to my father, he just shook his head in amazement. I was just as amazed as he was. God had proven Himself as my provider!

On my journey walking with the LORD Jesus, I was invited to Romania to speak at a pastors' conference. The Church there is exploding with growth. The LORD works in amazing ways.

A former Arab Palestinian from Israel, who came to the LORD through the witness of Gerald Derstine, had gone to Romania to have surgery for a goiter on his thyroid. While riding in a cab from the airport to his motel, he began talking to the cab driver about the LORD. The driver had not yet made a decision to give his heart to the LORD by the time they arrived at the motel. The driver discovered that he was unable to let go of the steering wheel. It seemed his hands were stuck to the wheel. He asked, "What is happening? Why am I unable to turn loose of the wheel?" The passenger told him, "The LORD wants to give you more time to make your decision." When the driver prayed to receive Jesus into his heart, suddenly and miraculously his hands were freed from the wheel. You may wonder why God would work this way. Listen to the rest of the story.

The driver was so filled with joy that he called his uncle Cornell Barcu, owner of the cab company, to tell him what had happened. Cornell had many doubts about this experience and he stated emphatically, "God does not do things like this anymore!" Upon his nephew's insistence, Cornell agreed to meet this man, so it was arranged. Before the evening was over, Cornell and his whole family were born again.

This missionary journey in my life, just like each mission trip I have been on, was another step God used to train me for the future ministry to which He has called me. Romania had been under the thumb of communism for many years, but the time had come for the Gospel of the Kingdom to come to them. In addition to conducting the pastors' seminar, we traveled around Romania to several of the newly established churches. We prayed with many Romanians to receive Christ.

In one church, there was a young man who had been born deaf and was unable to speak. [He was actually a pastor's son.] Our team prayed for him and the first word he cried out was, "JESUS!" He is now able to speak and hear.

In another church, I was asked to speak. Even though I had come down with a severe cold, I would not let that keep me from doing what I was sent there to do. I preached, and then we were going to pray for the people. I noticed a man come into the meeting using two crutches to walk. I wanted to pray for him. However, Edgar Miller from White Pigeon, Michigan, met him first. God works in such miraculous ways. I saw the need for healing of his legs, but God knew what he needed to be whole. Unknown to us, he was also deaf. We did not see a manifested healing that evening in his legs. Yet the next day this man got up early and walked several miles to the city where we were conducting the seminar to give thanks.

The interpreter related what had happened to this man and reported, "He actually had been deaf in both ears. He had had a dream the night before we went to that church to minister. In his dream, he saw an angel that looked exactly like Edgar Miller. The LORD spoke to him in the dream that if he would go to the church that evening, he would be healed. He was healed of the deafness and spent time later that night walking around listening to the dogs bark and all of the other sounds."

Just like the account of the ten lepers in the Bible where only one turned back to give thanks and was made completely whole, he had come to where we were meeting to give thanks and testify to what God had done. Praise the name of the LORD! Now I understood why Edgar Miller was to be the one to pray with him.

Everything we experience, every trial and every blessing, is working for our good to prepare us for the next opportunity we have to proclaim the message of the Kingdom.

Here is one more testimony from the Romanian trip. We went to a church where the community had suffered significant damage from recent floods. Several of the team members shared a short Word and then we divided up and went into the crowd to pray for the people. The men were sitting on one side and the women on the other side. One of the team prayed for a woman and then felt led to go and pray for a young man on the other side. This young man had been very skeptical but received the prayer. The language barrier made it impossible for the team to know what the people were saying without an interpreter.

Later, we received a report on the phone of one of the most amazing stories. That young man had been diagnosed as needing a kidney transplant.

His surgery was scheduled for the next morning. He had traveled for some distance to spend the night with his aunt who was going to donate one of her kidneys to him. (Earlier, this team member had prayed for this same woman.) After prayer that night, the young man was born again and healed. The next morning he went to the hospital for his appointment. He told the doctor what had happened and that he had been healed. The doctor did not believe him and wanted to proceed with the surgery. The man insisted, "No, I have been healed." He then got up, ran down the hall of the hospital, turned around and ran back. The doctor exclaimed, "You can't do this! You need surgery!" Finally, the doctor had to admit that God had healed him.

When this man returned to his village, another new church was birthed as he told his testimony all over town. This is how God is moving in Romania in this present day. Other miracles occurred in Romania, but let me move on to another step in my training journey.

Chapter 25

AFRICA—AT LAST

Earlier in my life, I had been unwilling to consent to becoming a missionary and going to Africa. Yet now God had changed my heart. I met Ebenezer Sefah from Ghana, Africa, at Christian Retreat during one of the annual minister convocations. He invited us to minister in his country. Shirley had not travelled with me on previous missionary journeys because we felt she was needed at the home base. This time we were determined to go together, and we did.

When we arrived in Accra, the capital city, we were met by Ebenezer and his driver. We packed all of our bags in his car although I could not believe it was possible. Our trip lasted about four hours over some rather rough roads. We arrived at his very nice home and enjoyed wonderful ministry during our stay. He and his wife, Margaret, were excellent hosts.

Ebenezer is the first-born son of a king in Ghana. This, of course, means he is a Prince, next in line to assume the office of King. However, when he became born again he told his father he could not become King, as tradition would dictate. His father was very disappointed. Yet over time, the King too became born again and likewise abdicated his kingship to his brother. I tell you this to explain why Ebenezer has such a firm grasp on Kingdom understanding. He shared a message with our church when he was in the United States entitled "A King is Bound by His Words." It was an awesome revelation. We who have been born in a democratic society have difficulty understanding Kingdom principles.

I preached at several meetings, and Shirley ministered at a ladies meeting. We also visited several homes where we prayed with families for individual needs. Ebenezer's influence provided us with an invitation to meet with the mayor of the second largest city in Ghana as well as the King in that area.

We took a side trip to the slave castle. There, many thousands of slaves had been held in deplorable conditions while they awaited the ships that brought them to America and other countries in the world. We walked into the dungeons where they had been held. Then we went to the huge gate that opened up where they had been loaded on the ships. A sign named that entry point, "The Gate of No Return." We had a tour guide who explained that there was a church directly above the dungeon. The slave traders would go to church there, no doubt able to hear screams coming out of the dungeon from the slaves. We came home with a different perspective due to the things we saw there.

I returned to Ghana in 2007 with Gerald Derstine for a convocation of ministers and to participate in the graduation exercises for their Bible school. It is such a privilege to travel with Gerald and learn from this great man of God. He has travelled all over the world preaching the Kingdom of God and establishing churches wherever he has gone.

Little known to me, I was about to face a different kind of challenge than I had ever faced before.

Chapter 26

NO PULSE!

Gerald and I flew back to New York and had a layover there. Early the next morning, on Wednesday, August 8, 2007, we had to rise early to get to the airport for a pre-dawn flight. Severe weather caused the airport to be closed for a couple of hours. They actually had tornado warnings posted. Gerald and I parted ways, as he was flying back to Minnesota by way of Chicago, and I was returning to South Carolina through Washington D.C.

I arrived in D.C. two hours late and had only thirty minutes to catch my next plane. I ran as fast as I could, but was soon out of breath. For the past six or eight months, I had noticed my breathing had become more challenged. I had even told Shirley that maybe I should get a physical checkup. However, I had kept putting it off.

I reached the security checkpoint totally out of breath. There was one party ahead of me, so I had to wait a moment for them to be cleared. I bent over as my chest heaved, trying to catch my breath. When I stood up, I was dizzy for what seemed about one-and-one half circles, and then the lights went out. When I awoke, there was an Emergency Medical Services worker kneeling beside me. I heard him ask someone, "Did you need to shock him?" Someone standing behind him answered, "Yes. We could find no pulse."

I remember thinking, "I believe they are talking about me!" They placed me on a stretcher and started to pick me up. I asked, "Where are we going?" They informed me we were going to take a short trip to the hospital. I responded, "I will miss my plane!" The truth is my plane had probably already gone.

I must have slipped in and out of consciousness as I remember only bits and pieces of what was actually happening. I do recall being loaded into the ambulance and a two or three minute ride to the hospital, but it must have taken longer than that. They sprayed nitro under my tongue twice on the way to the hospital. I remember being in the emergency room and asking if I could call Shirley because I was aware that she would be going to Savannah, Georgia, to pick me up from the airport.

When I arrived at the emergency room, they ran some tests. I was told that the aortic valve was eighty-five percent blocked. I was only operating on fifteen percent blood flow out of my heart. They advised me that I needed surgery immediately. I asked them if I could call my wife Shirley.

They dialed the phone and handed it to me. When Shirley answered, I asked her if she had already left to go to Savannah, Georgia, to pick me up at the airport. She explained that she was just getting ready to leave. Then I said, "You won't believe where I am." She responded, "Now what?"

I replied, "No, you don't understand. You won't believe where I am. I am in the emergency room at the hospital." I described what had happened and told her that they wanted to perform surgery.

She and our son, Tyler, packed some bags and headed for Washington D. C., arriving about 3:00 in the morning. They came immediately up to my room to see me for a little while before they went to the motel to get some sleep. The next day, more tests determined I had three or four blockages in other places around my heart. These could probably have been fixed with stints but they suggested a bypass procedure since they would be inside my chest anyway to replace the aortic valve. Friday morning they successfully performed the surgery.

I was released on Tuesday of the next week, just four days after the operation. They did not want me to travel or leave the area for a week in order to monitor my progress. I can testify and say that there was pain involved. Just getting into bed was a major undertaking.

They later told me that my heart had stopped from lack of oxygen, but I did not have a heart attack. I fell to the floor right where there was a defibrillator hanging on the wall. Someone, a pilot or a policeman, saw me fall and knew how to operate the defibrillator. They cut open the new shirt I had received as a special gift in Africa and shocked my heart to start it again. I wish I could have had the opportunity to thank those who worked on me but was unable to do so.

Our God is good. I had been healed again. Now I was looking forward to what God had in store for me next. I didn't need to wait long. I received another invitation to return to India to speak at the three ministries God had knitted to my heart.

Chapter 27

LUGGAGE LOST IN INDIA

This time I flew directly into Hyderabad. One truth we must know is that things do not always go as intended, especially on the mission field. Often, God has a better plan. I had scheduled to spend only two days there before traveling onward. However, I ended up staying four days and preaching twice on Sunday.

Next I traveled by bus to the city of Rajahmundry. When I got off the bus, I picked up my bag and loaded it into the car with Sharath for our journey to Razole. We had driven about forty-five minutes when Sharath's cell phone rang. The driver of the bus I had traveled on asked if I had taken the wrong bag. I immediately looked into the bag in my possession, and sure enough, I had someone else's bag. The bus driver actually said they would wait there until we returned to switch bags. Can you believe that? I had my video camera and other important things in that bag. When we arrived, there was my bag with every one of my things still in it. God is so good! We finally arrived in Razole where we experienced much fruitful ministry.

I preached on Sunday morning. When I gave the opportunity for people to respond to a call for salvation, a young couple came forward to give their hearts to the LORD. That afternoon we baptized them and one other who desired baptism in the nearby river. Water baptism in India is a major thing because many are cast out of their family for becoming Christian.

The couple invited us to their home for a meal that next week. They were from the scavenger community. That meant their people were of the caste who cleaned human waste from homes and septic tanks, not one of the most glamorous of chores, if you want to talk about the hierarchy of dirty jobs.

Sharath had gone to their community when the floods came to help them with food and essentials. That is what opened their hearts to come to church and hear the good news of the Kingdom of God. It was not even an accepted practice to go to that community. Nevertheless, God's love through Brother Sharath broke the traditions and brought salvation to the village.

We had a lovely meal with them and ended the evening with a worship service on the roof of their house. It was interesting to see the eyes of the neighbors peering out of the darkness as the music drew attention to the message we brought. My friend, this is true evangelism in action. This is how the Kingdom of God shall fill the whole earth as the water covers the sea, and then the end shall come.

Chapter 28

A MIRACLE IN HAITI

On February 23, 2010, I went on my first mission trip to Haiti. This was just after the January 13, 2010, earthquake. Our son, Tyler, went with me as our photographer. The devastation was beyond belief.

We went to take funds that people in the United States had contributed. Our mission team met directly with families and prayed with them. The scripture that God gave me to encourage them is found in Matthew 28:2, "And behold, a great earthquake had occurred, **for** an angel of the LORD descended from heaven and came and rolled away the stone and sat upon it." [Emphasis mine.]

I have noticed that when there is a great earthquake in some location in the world, a great revival follows. We know the Scripture tells us that angels are ministering spirits sent to assist the saints of God. I believe that the stronger the earthquake, the stronger the angel. I also visualize that each aftershock sends smaller angels following their head angel as his assistants. Therefore, I am expecting great revivals in Haiti as well as in Chile!

I can testify that the angel of the LORD was surely with us as we walked about neighborhoods totally destroyed by the earthquake. In one such neighborhood, there were completely collapsed houses and other homes, though almost still in an upright position, were broken beyond repair.

We visited some of the temporary dwellings in one neighborhood. People who lost their houses were living in a tent city. We walked into one such tent where we found an elderly woman lying on a mattress on the ground. Our interpreter told us that the women had been totally paralyzed even before the earthquake. When her home collapsed, her husband was killed leaving her completely helpless. There were no living family members to assist her.

I was instantly reminded of the man in Israel's Golan Heights who was lying on his bed dying. The team of believers there had prayed for him and then helped him stand to his feet. He had been miraculously healed. I told this woman that story through the interpreter and then asked, "Can we pray for you?"

She quickly agreed. We wasted no time laying hands on her while praying. There were no visible signs that anything had happened, but I spoke with confidence, "Now let's stand her up." We lifted her to her feet, though they still were turned sideways. I lifted my feet up, put them down and told her to do the same. She tried once, twice, and on the third time, it went better. I kept on encouraging her, and she kept trying, each time lifting them higher and higher. The smile on her face kept getting wider and wider.

She got tired quickly, so we sat her down on her bed. She repeatedly thrust out her arms, opening and closing her hands as she looked at them. She was speaking excitedly, but of course, I could not understand her.

I kept asking, "What is she saying? What is she saying?" Our interpreter never answered. I don't know if he was as excited as I was, but it really didn't matter at that point. Before we left, I asked her if she wanted to try standing again. She immediately stretched out her arms, as a little child would do in order to show us she wanted to get up. We lifted her to her feet, and again she started lifting her legs up and down.

When we left, she had a big grin on her face. Praise the LORD for His goodness and His miracle working power.

Chapter 29

WHAT'S NEXT?

I don't know all that God has in store for us in the future, but I am confident it will be good. I have had many dreams that have not yet been fulfilled.

I have seen the Great Wall of China in a dream and I fully expect God will send me there one day. I have dreamed about a young girl whose spine was outside her body with spina bifida or extreme scoliosis. She received healing when I laid hands on her.

I had a dream where I saw a man in a bright blue suit. He prophesied to me, "You will get to receive the evil one." I interpreted that to mean I will have the opportunity to lead a person to Jesus that many would consider extremely evil. I believe God showed me who that person is. I will know when the prophet in my dream actually gives the prophecy to me, because the prophet identified me by a specific phrase that I cannot share at this time. I do expect God will set up this meeting and send the prophet who will confirm this prophecy when the time is right.

I fully expect one day to see the dead rise. Why not? Does not your own Scripture say, "Heal the sick, cleanse the lepers, raise the dead, cast out demons. Freely you have received, freely give" (Mt 10:8)? Additionally, John 14:12 reaffirms, "Most assuredly, I say to you, he who believes in Me, the works that I do he will do also; and greater works than these he will do, because I go to My Father." Then again, Hebrews 13:8 proclaims, "Jesus Christ is the same yesterday, today, and forever."

My desire is that our children, their spouses, our grandchildren, great grandchildren and all who follow after us, will have as vibrant of a relationship with Jesus as we have found, and even more so. I pray that each one who reads this book will know the great joy that is found only in Jesus. I pray that those who have already invited Jesus into their lives will be challenged to draw closer to Him. I pray you will be filled with His Holy Spirit and empowered to fulfill your calling from Him. [I have reprinted a plan of salvation followed by how you can receive the Baptism in the Holy Spirit at the end of this book.]

You have read of how God spoke to us many times through dreams and visions. He is still speaking today. He speaks through His Word, the Bible. He speaks through other people. He speaks through books written by others. He speaks audibly. He even speaks through circumstances in your life. I believe He is speaking to you right now. How will you answer your call?

God is no respecter of persons. What He has done for Shirley and me, He will do for you. Do not expect that it will be exactly the same. Remember, you are an individual person with a unique personality and unique giftings. There are people in the world today that only you can reach. I challenge you to reach out. Call on God. Cast yourself totally and completely on Him. You can trust HIM to meet you and fulfill your every desire. He will answer you and show you great and mighty things that you know not.

May God Himself richly bless you!

Appendix 1

WHAT'S NEXT FOR YOU?

Following are the "Four Spiritual Laws" by Bill Bright. (Reprinted with permission.) Please take a moment to read them. If you pray the prayer of salvation, please tell someone. You are welcome to contact me. I will rejoice with you and the angels in Heaven. By telling someone, it will strengthen you and help you understand the reality of being born again.

Have You Heard of the **FOUR SPIRITUAL LAWS?**

Just as there are physical laws that govern the physical universe, so are there spiritual laws that govern your relationship with God.

LAW 1

God loves you and offers a wonderful plan for your life.

God's Love

"God so loved the world that He gave His one and only Son,
that whoever believes in Him shall not perish but have eternal life"
(John 3:16, NIV).

God's Plan

[Christ speaking] "I came that they might have life,
and might have it abundantly" [that it might be full and meaningful]
(John 10:10).

Why is it that most people are not experiencing that abundant life?

Because...

LAW 2

**Man is sinful and separated from God.
Therefore, he cannot know and experience
God's love and plan for his life.**

Man is Sinful

"All have sinned and fall short of the glory of God"
(Romans 3:23).

Man was created to have fellowship with God; but,
because of his own stubborn self-will, he chose to go his own
independent way and fellowship with God was broken.
This self-will, characterized by an attitude of active rebellion
or passive indifference, is an evidence of what the Bible calls sin.

Man is Separated

"The wages of sin is death" [spiritual separation from God]
(Romans 6:23).

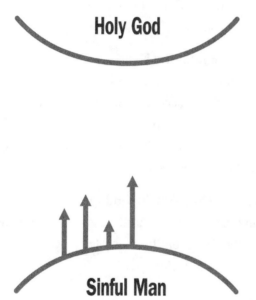

This diagram illustrates that God is holy and man is sinful. A great gulf separates the two. The arrows illustrate that man is continually trying to reach God and the abundant life through his own efforts, such as a good life, philosophy, or religion—but he inevitably fails. The third law explains the only way to bridge this gulf...

Law 3

Jesus Christ is God's only provision for man's sin. Through Him you can know and experience God's love and plan for your life.

He Died in Our Place

"God demonstrates His own love toward us, in that while we were yet sinners, Christ died for us"
(Romans 5:8).

He Rose from the Dead

"Christ died for our sins... He was buried...
He was raised on the third day, according to the Scriptures...
He appeared to Peter, then to the twelve.
After that He appeared to more than five hundred..."
(I Corinthians 15:3–6).

He is the Only Way to God

"Jesus said to him, 'I am the way, and the truth, and the life, no one comes to the Father but through Me'"
(John 14:6).

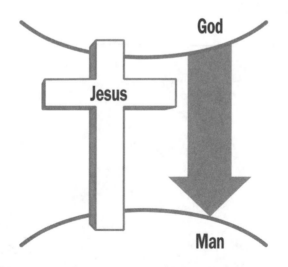

This diagram illustrates that God has bridged the gulf that separates us from Him by sending His Son, Jesus Christ, to die on the cross in our place to pay the penalty for our sins. It is not enough just to know these three laws...

LAW 4

**We must individually receive Jesus Christ as Savior and LORD;
then we can know and experience God's love and plan for our lives.**

We Must Receive Christ
"As many as received Him, to them He gave the right to become children
of God, even to those who believe in His name"
(John 1:12).

We Receive Christ through Faith
"By grace you have been saved through faith; and that not of yourselves,
it is the gift of God; not as result of works that no one should boast"
(Ephesians 2:8,9).

When We Receive Christ, We Experience a New Birth
(Read John 3:1–8.)

We Receive Christ through Personal Invitation
[Christ speaking] "Behold, I stand at the door and knock;
if any one hears My voice and opens the door, I will come in to him"
(Revelation 3:20).

Receiving Christ involves turning to God from self (repentance)
and trusting Christ to come into our lives to forgive our sins
and to make us what He wants us to be.
Just to agree **intellectually** that Jesus Christ is the Son of God
and that He died on the cross for our sins is not enough.
Nor is it enough to have an **emotional** experience.
We receive Jesus Christ by **faith**, as an act of the **will**.

Two Kinds of Lives

These two circles represent two kinds of lives.

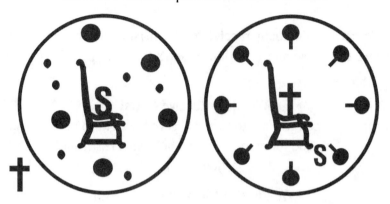

Self-Directed Life

S   Self is on the throne

✝   Christ is outside the life

●   Interests are directed by self, often resulting in discord and frustration

Christ-Directed Life

✝   Christ is in the life and on the throne

S   Self is yielding to Christ, resulting in harmony with God's plan

●   Interests are directed by Christ, resulting in harmony with God's plan

Which circle best represents your life?
Which circle would you like to have represent your life?
The following explains how you can receive Christ:

You Can Receive Christ Right Now by Faith through Prayer
(Prayer is talking with God)

God knows your heart and is not so concerned with your words as He is with the attitude of your heart. The following is a suggested prayer:

Lord Jesus, I need You. Thank You for dying on the cross for my sins. I open the door of my life and receive You as my Savior and Lord. Thank You for forgiving my sins and giving me eternal life. Take control of the throne of my life. Make me the kind of person You want me to be.

Does This Prayer Express the Desire of Your Heart?

If it does, I invite you to pray this prayer right now, and Christ will come into your life, as He promised.

How to Know That Christ is in Your Life?

Did you receive Christ into your life? According to His promise in Revelation 3:20, where is Christ right now in relation to you? Christ said that He would come into your life. Would He mislead you? On what authority do you know that God has answered your prayer? (The trustworthiness of God Himself and His Word.)

The Bible Promises Eternal Life to All Who Receive Christ

"God has given us eternal life, and this life is in His Son. He who has the Son has the life; he who does not have the Son of God does not have the life" (I John 5:11–13).

Thank God often that Christ is in your life and that He will never leave you (Hebrews 13:5). You can know on the basis of His promise that Christ lives in you and that you have eternal life from the very moment you invite Him in. He will not deceive you.

An important reminder...

Do Not Depend on Feelings

The promise of God's Word, the Bible—not our feelings—is our authority. The Christian lives by faith (trust) in the trustworthiness of God Himself and His Word. This train diagram illustrates the relationship among **fact** (God and His Word), **faith** (our trust in God and His Word), and **feeling** (the result of our faith and obedience) (John 14:21).

The train will run with or without a caboose. However, it would be useless to attempt to pull the train by the caboose. In the same way, as Christians we do not depend on feelings or emotions, but we place our faith (trust) in the trustworthiness of God and the promises of His Word.

Now That You Have Received Christ

The moment you received Christ by faith, as an act of the will, many things happened, including the following:

- Christ came into your life (Revelation 3:20; Colossians 1:27).

- Your sins were forgiven (Colossians 1:14).

- You became a child of God (John 1:12).

- You received eternal life (John 5:24).

- You began the great adventure for which God created you (John 10:10; 2 Corinthians 5:17; 1 Thessalonians 5:18).

Can you think of anything more wonderful that could happen to you than receiving Christ? Would you like to thank God in prayer right now for what He has done for you? By thanking God, you demonstrate your faith.

To enjoy your new life to the fullest...

Suggestions for Christian Growth

Spiritual growth results from trusting Jesus Christ. "The righteous man shall live by faith" (Galatians 3:11). A life of faith will enable you to trust God increasingly with every detail of your life, and to practice the following:

G *Go* to God in prayer daily (John 15:7).

R *Read* God's Word daily (Acts 17:11); begin with the Gospel of John.

O *Obey* God moment by moment (John 14:21).

W *Witness* for Christ by your life and words (Matthew 4:19; John 15:8).

T *Trust* God for every detail of your life (1 Peter 5:7).

H *Holy Spirit*—allow Him to control and empower your daily life and witness (Galatians 5:16, 17; Acts 1:8; Ephesians 5:18).

Fellowship in a Good Church

God's Word instructs us not to forsake "the assembling of ourselves together" (Hebrews 10:25). Several logs burn brightly together; but put one aside on the cold hearth and the fire goes out. So it is with your relationship with other Christians.

If you do not belong to a church, do not wait to be invited. Take the initiative; call the pastor of a nearby church where Christ is honored and His Word is preached. Start this week, and make plans to attend regularly.

Appendix 2

HOW TO RECEIVE THE BAPTISM IN THE HOLY SPIRIT—WHAT TO EXPECT WHEN YOU DO

As I have said in the previous chapters, when God asked me, **"Do you see what I can do if you will just go?"** I said, "Yes, LORD, I will go." I took off all restraints.

1. The first thing you must do to receive the Baptism in the Holy Spirit is to take off all restraints by fully surrendering to God and His will for your life.

2. Ask Jesus to baptize you in the Holy Spirit. You see, water baptism is for repentance, the forgiveness of sins. Holy Spirit baptism is for power, power to be a witness. Matthew 3:11 says, "I indeed baptize you with water unto repentance, but He who is coming after me is mightier than I, whose sandals I am not worthy to carry. He will **baptize you with the Holy Spirit and fire.**" [Emphasis mine.]

3. Why does Jesus baptize us in the Holy Spirit? It is so we can receive power and boldness to be witnesses. Acts 1:8 states, "But you shall receive power when the Holy Spirit has come upon you; and you shall be witnesses to Me in Jerusalem, and in all Judea and Samaria, and to the end of the earth." You will receive power, boldness and confidence to witness for Jesus. Here's a great example in the lives of the disciples, not long after the Holy Spirit fell on the Day of Pentecost.

> The next day the rulers, elders and teachers of the law met in Jerusalem.
> Annas the high priest was there, and so were Caiaphas, John, Alexander and the other men of the high priest's family.
> They had Peter and John brought before them and began to question them: "By what power or what name did you do this?"
> Then **Peter, filled with the Holy Spirit**, said to them: "Rulers and elders of the people!
> If we are being called to account today for an act of kindness shown to a cripple and are asked how he was healed, then know this, you and all the people of Israel: It is by the name of Jesus Christ of Nazareth, whom you crucified but whom

God raised from the dead, that this man stands before you healed.

He is the stone you builders rejected, which has become the capstone.

Salvation is found in no one else, for there is no other name under heaven given to men by which we must be saved."

When they saw the courage (the boldness-KJV) of Peter and John and realized that they were unschooled, ordinary men, they were astonished and they took note that these men had been with Jesus.

But since they could see the man who had been healed standing there with them, there was nothing they could say.

So they ordered them to withdraw from the Sanhedrin and then conferred together. "What are we going to do with these men?" they asked. "Everybody living in Jerusalem knows they have done an outstanding miracle, and we cannot deny it.

But to stop this thing from spreading any further among the people, we must warn these men to speak no longer to anyone in this name."

Then they called them in again and commanded them not to speak or teach at all in the name of Jesus.

But Peter and John replied, "Judge for yourselves whether it is right in God's sight to obey you rather than God.

For we cannot help speaking about what we have seen and heard." [Emphasis mine.]   (Acts 4:5–20)

4. What will happen when I receive the Baptism in the Holy Spirit? Let's see what happened when the Holy Spirit fell in the upper room ten days after Jesus ascended into Heaven.

When the Day of Pentecost had fully come, they were all with one accord in one place.

And suddenly there came a sound from heaven, as of a rushing mighty wind, and it filled the whole house where they were sitting.

Then there appeared to them divided tongues, as of fire, and one sat upon each of them.

And they were all filled with the Holy Spirit and began to speak with other tongues, as the Spirit gave them utterance. [Emphasis mine.]   (Acts 2:1–4)

5.   Must I speak in tongues when I receive the Baptism in the Holy Spirit? The simple answer is that God does not force us to do anything. When you receive the gift of the Holy Spirit, you receive the ability to speak in tongues and you may do that if you choose to, but it will be your decision. I Corinthians 14:32 says, "The spirits of prophets are **subject to the control** of prophets" (NIV). [Emphasis mine.]

6.   Didn't tongues pass away with the apostles? In Acts, we see Peter speaking to the Gentiles some time after the day of Pentecost.

> *Then Peter opened his mouth and said: "In truth I perceive that God shows no partiality.*
>
> *But in every nation whoever fears Him and works righteousness is accepted by Him.*
>
> *The word which God sent to the children of Israel, preaching peace through Jesus Christ—He is LORD of all—*
>
> *That word you know, which was proclaimed throughout all Judea, and began from Galilee after the baptism which John preached:*
>
> *How God anointed Jesus of Nazareth with the Holy Spirit and with power, who went about doing good and healing all who were oppressed by the devil, for God was with Him.*
>
> *And we are witnesses of all things which He did both in the land of the Jews and in Jerusalem, whom they killed by hanging on a tree.*
>
> *Him God raised up on the third day, and showed Him openly, not to all the people, but to witnesses chosen before by God, even to us who ate and drank with Him after He arose from the dead.*
>
> *And He commanded us to preach to the people, and to testify that it is He who was ordained by God to be Judge of the living and the dead.*

To Him all the prophets witness that, through His name, whoever believes in Him will receive remission of sins."

*While Peter was still speaking these words, **the Holy Spirit fell upon all those who heard the word.***

And those of the circumcision who believed were astonished, as many as came with Peter, because the gift of the Holy Spirit had been poured out on the Gentiles also.

For they heard them speak with tongues and magnify God.

*Then Peter answered, "Can anyone forbid water, that these should not be baptized who have **received the Holy Spirit <u>just as we have</u>?"***

And he commanded them to be baptized in the name of the LORD. Then they asked him to stay a few days. [Emphasis mine.]

(Acts 10:34–48)

7. Didn't I receive everything when I was saved? Again, I refer to the Scripture where the answer seems to be, "No."

Paul stayed on in Corinth for some time. Then he left the brothers and sailed for Syria, accompanied by Priscilla and Aquila. Before he sailed, he had his hair cut off at Cenchrea because of a vow he had taken.

***They arrived at Ephesus, where Paul left Priscilla and Aquila.** He himself went into the synagogue and reasoned with the Jews.*

When they asked him to spend more time with them, he declined.

But as he left, he promised, "I will come back if it is God's will." Then he set sail from Ephesus.

When he landed at Caesarea, he went up and greeted the church and then went down to Antioch.

After spending some time in Antioch, Paul set out from there and traveled from place to place throughout the region of Galatia and Phrygia, strengthening all the disciples.

*Meanwhile a **Jew named Apollos**, a native of Alexandria, came to Ephesus. **He was a learned man, with a thorough knowledge of the Scriptures.***

He had been instructed in the way of the Lord, and he spoke with great fervor and taught about Jesus <u>accurately</u>, though he knew only the baptism of John.

*He began to speak boldly in the synagogue. When Priscilla and Aquila heard him, they invited him to their home and **explained to him the way of God <u>more adequately</u>.***

When Apollos wanted to go to Achaia, the brothers encouraged him and wrote to the disciples there to welcome him. On arriving, he was a great help to those who by grace had believed.

For he vigorously refuted the Jews in public debate, proving from the Scriptures that Jesus was the Christ.

*While Apollos was at Corinth, **<u>Paul</u>** took the road through the interior and arrived at **<u>Ephesus</u>**. There he **found some disciples** and asked them, "Did you receive the Holy Spirit when you believed?" They answered, **"No, we have not even heard that there is a Holy Spirit."***

So Paul asked, "Then what baptism did you receive?" "John's baptism," they replied.

Paul said, "John's baptism was a baptism of repentance. He told the people to believe in the one coming after him, that is, in Jesus."

On hearing this, they were baptized in the name of the Lord Jesus.

When Paul placed his hands on them, the Holy Spirit came on them, and they spoke in tongues and prophesied.

There were about twelve men in all. [Emphasis mine.]

(Acts 18:18–19:7, NIV)

Let me encourage you to pray right now and ask Jesus to baptize you in His Holy Spirit.... Now just begin to praise His wonderful name.

There is so much more. And if you will seek all that God has for you, He will let you find Him!

Please contact me if I can help you any further.

Thank you.

Available for speaking engagements

Contact Information:
Pastor Tom Nafziger
c/o Christian Retreat
1200 Glory Way Blvd.
Bradenton, FL 34212
E-mail: cffpastor@yahoo.com
Cell: 803-571-0784
Christian Retreat Switchboard: 941-746-2882

Other Books Published by

Deeper Revelation Books

Producing sound and edifying teaching materials for the body of Christ.

Publishing loving presentations of Biblical truth to followers of other worldviews.

───◆───

See the following six pages

For more information visit www.deeperrevelationbooks.org

Are you a Christian author?
Have you written a book? Are you looking for a publisher?

Get in touch with Deeper Revelation Books!
We come alongside, as your "co-visionary" and "co-publisher," to help you produce a product of excellence and distribute it worldwide. This may be your answer.

Contact us today: 423-478-2843 or info@deeperrevelationbooks.org

God's Strategy for Tragedy

A Documented Modern-day Miracle
by Ben Godwin

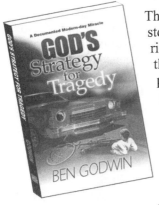

This book is a faith builder! Read the riveting, true story of Ben Godwin who was struck by a car while riding a bicycle at age seven. The collision dislodged three inches of bone from his left leg. Doctors prescribed bone graft surgery and predicted a permanently crippled limb. Then God intervened. The bone was restored by a creative miracle (proven by before-and-after x-rays). Ever since, Ben has enjoyed "a miracle walk on a miracle leg, serving in a miracle ministry."

- Do miracles still happen today?
- Why does God allow tragedy?
- How should we respond to tragedy?
- How can you receive a miracle?

This book provides solid answers to these and other questions and illustrates, both from the Scriptures and real life, how God can turn tragedy into a testimony.

ISBN: 978-0-942507-45-4 **—Price: $14.99**

BEN GODWIN, B.Th., began preaching at age thirteen and has been in full-time ministry since 1987. He presently serves as pastor of the Goodsprings Full Gospel Church near Birmingham, Alabama, and hosts a weekly television program called "The Word Workshop." Ben and his wife, Michelle, work as a team in ministry. They and their three children, Nathan, Emily and Noah reside in Goodspring, Alabama.

www.bengodwin.org

Raised from the Dead

A True Account
by Richard Madison

After a horrible car accident, Richard Madison was pronounced dead-on-arrival. His family was told three times to make funeral arrangements. God revealed Himself to Richard through an out-of-body experience, and ten weeks later he walked out of a wheelchair. He is now a walking miracle testimony to thousands of people throughout the world that God's love can powerfully restore even the most hopeless lives. This amazing book will build your faith.

ISBN: 978-0-942507-43-0   **—Price: $13.95**

"Jesus walked into that hospital room, and laid His hand on Rick Madison's head and healed him."   —Pat Robertson

"Fast living led to a dead end, but a new life began with an out-of-body experience."   —Ben Kinchlow

"Richard, you've had everything go wrong that could go wrong and ...you are a living miracle."

—Dr. Kenneth Sharp
Vanderbilt University Medical Center

RICHARD MADISON is a full-time evangelist who travels the world to tell the remarkable story of how God raised him from his deathbed and completely delivered him from drugs and alcohol. Richard is a highly sought after speaker with a powerful healing and prophetic ministry. He and his family live in Oakman, Alabama.

www.rickmadison.com

Authentic Enlightenment

The inspirational story of a spiritual seeker
by Vail Carruth

Transcendental Meditation still attracts many seekers to its beliefs and practices. Vail Carruth was one of the "originals", joining this group shortly after its introduction in the U.S. In *Authentic Enlightenment* she candidly explains why she was drawn to TM in the early 60s and how she advanced to the point of becoming a certified teacher.

Referred to as a "scientific relaxation technique," TM seemed to bring some benefits. However, this yoga discipline primarily served to turn Vail inward. Though it calmed the senses and opened her to supernatural experiences, still there was something missing. She finally concluded that these techniques would never be able to fill the emptiness of her heart or satisfy her thirst for God.

Vail's spiritual journey took a new direction when she called on the Name above all names—the Name of JESUS. It was only then that she experienced the reality of the HOLY SPIRIT and the unspeakable joy of GOD'S LOVE. Read her story and you, too, will be guided into transformation and wholeness in your life.

ISBN: 978-0-942507-42-3   **—Price: $15.95**

VAIL CARRUTH holds a BA in Fine Art from the University of California, Berkeley, and studied piano at the San Francisco Conservatory of Music. She is a former teacher of TM who shares her experiences in the movement with diverse audiences. Vail is also an artist, even in the way she paints a picture with her words. Her sole desire is to exalt her Creator and to make Him known to others.

www.living-light.net

God's Promises for your Children

A Guide to Intercession for Parents

by Mike Shreve

Parenting can really be challenging—sometimes overwhelming. But GOD is on your side! He has given 64 BIBLICAL PROMISES concerning your children—things He pledges to do for them—if you pray and believe.

Scripture declares He is "the faithful God who keeps covenant and mercy to a thousand generations..." (Dt. 7:9). How amazing! Biblically, a "generation" is probably forty years long. Now multiply that by a thousand. That's how long God promises to hover over your family line to manifest covenant provision and merciful care—all because YOU have made a genuine commitment to love and serve Him. Covenant and mercy—those are just two things God pledges to do for your offspring. There are 62 more promises showcased in this prayer devotional.

If you are a parent looking for hope, looking for encouragement, looking for a way out of the storm, looking for a miracle in your family—this is it! This is a revelation that really has the power to change everything!

ISBN: 978-0-942507-05-78   **—Price 14.99**

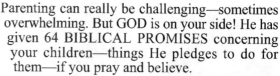

MIKE SHREVE, B.Th.,D.D., has been teaching God's Word since 1971. He is the author of ten books, three Bible studies, and is the founder of "Deeper Revelation Books." He is greatly blessed with a devoted wife, Elizabeth, who assists him in ministry, and two wonderful children, Zion Seth and Destiny Hope, who are both miracles from God.

www.shreveministries.org

Babylon or Jerusalem

Which Will Rule the World?
by Jan Willem van der Hoeven

Two cities figure predominantly in the Bible's discussion of the end times: BABYLON and JERUSALEM. One represents man's attempt to make a perfect world on his own; the other, God's intervention and salvation. One symbolizes man's drive for prosperity, stability and unity without God; the other, God's impartation of these things through submission to His Lordship.

One is a city full of greed, materialism and immmorality; the other, a city filled with self-lessness, peace, and holiness. One is the seat of a cruel megalomaniac: a world dictator who talks of peace and prosperity, but will finally be revealed as a false messiah. The other is the seat of the true Prince of Peace, whose reign will bring ultimate peace and righteousness to this world.

ISBN: 978-0-942507-82-9   **—Price: $15.99**

JAN WILLEM VAN DER HOEVEN is the founder/director of the International Christian Zionist Center in Israel. He was born in Holland and studied in England, obtaining his Bachelor of Divinity from London University.

Jan Willem's home for many years has been the Middle East, first in the Arab world, then in Israel. He was one of the initiators of the yearly, international, Christian celebration of the Feast of Tabernacles in Jerusalem and a principal founder of the International Christian Embassy. He has traveled extensively in many nations, addressing, Christian, Jewish and secular audiences, and is a recognized authority on the history, challenges and prophecies regarding this most strategic region of the world. Jan Willem and his wife, Ellen, live north of Jerusalem in Anatot, the Biblical home of Jeremiah the prophet.

www.israelmybeloved.com

Ordering Information

For a listing of other available books please visit our website:

www.deeperrevelationbooks.org

or call: 1-423-478-2843

Wholesalers and retailers should contact Anchor Distributors
or Baker &Taylor Distributors at their respective websites:

www.anchordistributors.com

www.btol.com

Individuals desiring these books should send the amount below,
(be sure to include your complete shipping information with
P.O. Box or street address, etc)
plus $5.00 s/h per book to:

Deeper Revelation Books

P.O. Box 4260

Cleveland, TN 37320-4260

You may also order online.

	QTY	PRICE	AMOUNT
GOD'S STRATEGY FOR TRAGEDY		$14.99	
RAISED FROM THE DEAD		$13.95	
AUTHENTIC ENLIGHTENMENT		$15.95	
GOD'S PROMISES FOR YOUR CHILDREN		$14.99	
BABYLON OR JERUSALEM		$15.99	
(Add $5.00 s/h per book)		TOTAL AMOUNT	